E NOTE

F AMERICA

G 23085640 A

WASHINGTON, D.C. 7

SERIES
1988

Secretary of the Treasury.

G 11

THE ASSOCIATED PRESS BOOK OF

THE WORLD'S RICHEST PEOPLE

CHET CURRIER

ARCH CAPE PRESS

NEW YORK

Text and Captions
Chet Currier

Photography
The Associated Press

Design
Clive Dorman
Claire Leighton

Commissioning Editor
Andrew Preston

Commissioning
Edward Doling
Laura Potts

Editorial
Gillian Waugh

Production
Ruth Arthur
Sally Connolly
David Proffit
Andrew Whitelaw

Director of Production
Gerald Hughes

CLB 2493
© 1991 Colour Library Books Ltd, Godalming, Surrey, England.
All rights reserved.
This 1991 edition published by Arch Cape Press,
distributed by Outlet Book Company, Inc., a Random House Company,
225 Park Avenue South, New York, New York 10003.
Color separations by Scantrans Pte Ltd, Singapore.
Printed and bound in Italy - by Milanostampa S.p.A. - Farigliano (CN)
ISBN 0 517 02013 0
8 7 6 5 4 3 2 1

CONTENTS

I'm opposed to millionaires," said the renowned novelist and humorist Mark Twain, "but it would be dangerous to offer me the position."

A century or so after that remark was made, it still holds true as an apt summation of the feelings that stir among most members of the human race when they contemplate the prospect of great wealth. If an editor were going to modernize Twain's observation at all, the only change necessary would be the substitution of "billionaires" for "millionaires," to take into account the incredible prosperity the twentieth century has brought to many parts of the world, and to adjust for that pernicious evil, inflation.

The rich may inspire in the rest of us admiration, envy, or even disgust; they almost always fascinate. It may be true, as some commentators have argued, that the just-completed 1980s constituted an era of abnormal emphasis on money, an age that briefly glorified materialism and then dismissed it as a philosophical and moral dead end. But if we are losing our enthusiasm for the pursuit of enlightened self-interest, why is capitalism driving out communism so dramatically in so many places these days? The epoch of economics may barely have begun.

The pages that follow present word-and-picture snapshots of more than fifty of the richest people on earth. This is by no means a comprehensive collection, which would require a book too big to hold in your hands. Rather, it is presented as a representative cross-section, chosen not only for geographical diversity but also for differences in manner, method and style.

A primary source of information for this book has been the annual rankings of the world's richest people compiled by the American magazines *Forbes* and *Fortune*. Both publications do an admirable job of chronicling the pursuit of wealth as both an ancient undertaking in deadly earnest and an entertaining spectator sport.

ROYALTY

SHIEKH JABER AHMED AL SABAH

EMIR OF KUWAIT

Kuwait – a little country measuring about 150 kilometers from border to border – is a wealthy country. In its small niche between Iran and Saudi Arabia on the Persian Gulf, it sits atop more than 10% of the world's reserves of oil. Generally, Kuwaitis get free education, health care and social services, without having to bother paying income tax.

Of course, some are richer than others. Far and away the wealthiest is Shiekh Jaber Ahmed Al Sabah, who, until the Iraqi invasion of 1990, was the latest in an unbroken line of two hundred years to rule the country as its emir. The government's assets comprise almost all of the local petroleum industry, plus enormous investments in the United States and elsewhere that it has made with its accumulated oil earnings. *Fortune* magazine estimates the net worth of the Shiekh's family holdings at $4.5 billion.

By all accounts, Jaber, in his mid-sixties, has never gone in much for the indulgences of the idle rich. Through his adult life he has served in a wide range of the appointive ministry positions that are responsible for the day-to-day operations of the government. His palace, while comfortable, is described as modest by the standards of many other royal residences around the world. In Kuwait there are at least three other families in the billionaire class, having built their fortunes on activities like real estate, construction and banking.

Kuwait was impoverished before the oil money came, and it could conceivably become so again after the oil money is gone. Jaber and other prominent Kuwaitis have pursued a variety of ventures to help their prosperity diversify and endure. A notable challenge: promoting agriculture in a nation almost devoid of natural sources of fresh water.

Above: the Emir of Kuwait at the Elysée Palace with French President Mitterand in 1989.

Facing page: (top) oil rigs in the open desert several miles west of Ahmadi, and (bottom) the Emir of Kuwait arriving in Rabat, Morocco, for an Arab summit meeting in 1974.

Hassan II

KING OF MOROCCO

Right: King Hassan II sitting for a portrait at the Royal Palace in Rabat in 1961.

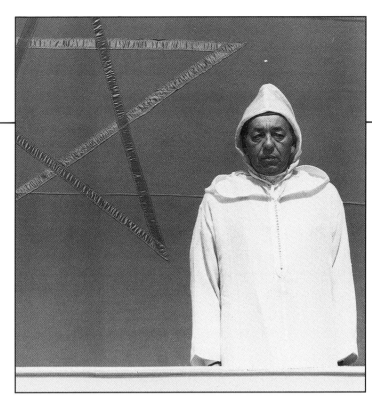

Right: King Hassan II at the Royal Palace in Marrakech during the commemoration of the 25th anniversary of his accession to the throne. Below: King Hassan II accompanied by his two sons, Mouslay Rachid (left) and Sidi Mohammed at the opening of a new dam at Sidi Cheho in 1975. In the background (center) is Kurt Waldheim, then UN Secretary General.

For their wealth and prominence, many billionaires pay a steep price in safety and peace of mind. They become targets, whether for well-intentioned charity fund-raisers or amoral opportunists. In cases where the riches are accompanied by political power, the perils are multiplied further.

No better proof of this principle can be found than Hassan II, King of Morocco, who has survived a series of attempted assassinations in the nearly thirty years since he succeeded his father, Muhammad V, on the throne of his African nation. Hassan, now in his early sixties, is said to be blessed with

baraka, a charmed life. At times he has had to supplement luck with pluck.

There was the incident in 1972, for instance, when air force fighter planes involved in a would-be coup fired on Hassan's jet as it brought him home from Paris. He bluffed his way down to a safe landing with a sham radio message, masquerading as a member of his crew, declaring that he had suffered mortal wounds.

The ruse worked long enough for him to make his escape once the plane was on the ground.

Above: the royal palace of King Hassan II in Fez, site of the 12th Arab Summit in 1981.

Right: King Hassan II with his family in 1987: (left to right) Princess Lalla Hasna, Crown Prince Sidi Mohammed, Princess Lalla Merien, Prince Mouslay Rachid and Princess Lalla Asmaa.

Facing page top: King Hassan II (right) meeting with Israeli Prime Minister Shimon Peres in Morocco in 1986, the first time an Israeli prime minister had visited an Arab country other than Egypt. Facing page bottom: Palestine Liberation Organisation Chairman Yassir Arafat (left) walks with King Hassan II upon Arafat's arrival in Casablanca for a meeting of the Arab League in 1989.

With such exploits has he paid part of the dues of a luxurious life that includes assets worth some $1.3 billion. In addition to his palaces in Morocco, these include real estate in Paris, New York and New Jersey. Though his reign has been punctuated by political instability, he is credited with significant efforts to improve his country's circumstances. He wrote its first constitution, adopted in 1962, and has built many schools, undertaken projects to irrigate desert land and expanded Moroccan industry in such endeavors as mining.

Below: Moroccan ladies throw flowers to King Hassan II during his silver jubilee commemoration in 1986.

Facing page: King Hassan II riding on horseback at the Royal Palace in Marrakech during ceremonies of allegiance in 1986.

MUDA HASSANAL BOLKIAH

THE SULTAN OF BRUNEI

Administrative buildings in
Bandar Seri Begawan,
Brunei.

Sultan Hassanal Bolkiah is crowned by his father Sir Omar Ali Suifuddin during a coronation ceremony that glistened with gold in the oil-rich sultanate.

At the northern edge of Malaysia, across the South China Sea from Vietnam, lies the small nation of Brunei, a longtime British protectorate that gained full independence in 1984. It has modest farming, forestry and fishing industries, and a rich store of offshore oil and gas deposits, first discovered in 1929.

Thanks in large measure to this last asset, Sir Muda Hassanal Bolkiah, Brunei's ruling sultan since 1967, commands a fortune worth some $25 billion. According to the best efforts of some diligent researchers, that makes him the world's wealthiest person by a margin of $7 billion or so. Of that, some $20 billion is invested overseas.

Most of Brunei's population of slightly more than 250,000 shares in the general wealth as well. They get free education and free medical care, and about half the workforce is employed by the government. The sultan, still in his mid-forties, is slated to rule for life. In addition to his financial assets, he is rich in domestic companionship, with two wives and nine children.

The sultan attracted some unaccustomed negative publicity when a $10 million contribution of his money turned up as an element in the mid-1980s political stir known in the United States as the Iran-Contra affair. A longer-term challenge facing the sultan and his subjects: how to set themselves up sufficiently to keep their living standard high after the oil and gas revenues run dry.

Above: Sultan Hassanal Bolkiah wearing the uniform of commander of the armed forces during a welcoming ceremony for Britain's Prince Charles in 1984. Right: Sultan Hassanal Bolkiah of Brunei with his queen on a state visit to Japan in 1984, welcomed by Emperor Hirohito.

Bandar Seri Begawan,
Brunei.

FAHD IBN ABD AL-AZIZ AL SAUD

KING OF SAUDI ARABIA

Right: an oil terminal in Saudi Arabia.

Facing page: (top) King Fahd and (bottom) the royal palace in Riyadh.

Fahd, king and prime minister of Saudi Arabia since 1982, owes much of his regal fortune of $20 billion or so to oil – the asset that catapulted his once-backward nation to world economic power in the course of just a few generations. He has served in various government positions since 1953, when he was barely thirty years old and, though sometimes described as moody, he is known for his quick wit and generous nature.

All has not been calm and prosperity in Saudi Arabia over the past few years. After soaring in the 1970s, oil prices endured some turbulent periods of decline in the '80s. There have also been outbreaks of civil and religious unrest. These tremors, however, seem to have

caused scarcely a crack in Fahd's demeanor or his sumptuous surroundings.

Indeed, it is reported that his family once worried a great deal about some of his extravagances, which included a penchant for parties, gambling on the French Riviera and hobnobbing with the Western jet set. Today, his ample girth and double chin still attest to a bounteous appetite.

Fahd's main residence, the vast Al-Yamamah ("Good Fortune") Palace in Riyadh, was four years in the building before its completion in 1987. His real estate portfolio includes at least a half-

The splendid facade of the Riyadh guest palace.

Prince Faisal Bin Fahd of Saudi Arabia escorting Princess Lilian of Sweden to the 1985 Nobel prize banquet in Stockholm at which the prince was a special guest of the Nobel Foundation.

King Fahd on a state visit to Britain, with Queen Elizabeth II, Queen Elizabeth the Queen Mother and Prince Philip. The Queen wore the chain of the Order of King Abdul Aziz in King Fahd's honor.

King Fahd reviewing the guard of honor in Cairo with President Hosni Mubarak of Egypt before holding talks in 1989.

Far left: King Fahd with former Vice President George Bush in Washington, D.C., in 1985, (left) with former President Reagan and Nancy Reagan on the same visit and (below left) the King with former British Prime Minister Margaret Thatcher on a visit in 1987.

dozen other estates from Casablanca to Geneva and London. To travel back and forth among these ports of call, the king can choose to take his 500-foot yacht, with built-in mosque, or his personal Boeing 747 jet, equipped with such extras as a banquet room and compasses that point toward the Moslem holy city of Mecca at all times.

Fahd's aides take pains to point out to visitors that Al-Yamamah was built not just for him, but for future generations of Saudi rulers. The success of King Fahd's efforts to steer the country into the twenty-first century, when oil might not produce so much economic power, will go a long way toward determining just how comfortably they occupy the throne.

ELIZABETH II
QUEEN OF ENGLAND

Queen Elizabeth II in the Throne Room at Buckingham Palace, wearing the Imperial State Crown, her Parliamentary Robe, and the Jubilee Necklace, made for Queen Victoria's Golden Jubilee.

Whenever they hear Queen Elizabeth II described as the richest woman in the world, many of her subjects and other admirers object. True, the assets of $10 billion-plus at her command fully qualify her for that designation. But the circumstances of the queen and her household represent a special case. Indeed, while *Fortune* magazine ranks her and her family among the five wealthiest people and families anywhere on earth, rival *Forbes* declines to include her and other royalty in its pantheon.

Both sides in this debate can make a credible case. An outside observer might not realize that some of the main properties in the Queen's life – such as Buckingham Palace and Windsor Castle

Above left: Queen Elizabeth II and the Duke of Edinburgh at Balmoral Castle, Scotland, in 1976, and (left) the Queen receiving congratulations from well-wishers during her silver jubilee celebrations in 1977.

– are owned by her country, not her family. Much else under her stewardship comes to her by direct virtue of the public position she holds. On the other hand, some say, to exclude her from a book like this one would mean omitting a picture of wealth put to use in a very stately way – and overlooking an example of how skillfully and judiciously a fortune can be managed.

For one thing, many regard Elizabeth as an exemplar of moderation and restraint. In her wardrobe, to cite one example, she has never sought to make "bold" statements or changes, sometimes to the frustration of the fashion industry. Biographers Graham

Above: members of the British Royal Family in the grounds of Balmoral Castle in 1979, and (left) the Queen reviewing the Yeomen of the Guard.

Facing page: the Queen at the 1985 state opening of Parliament.

and Heather Fisher have described her as "a fabulously wealthy woman with a strong economic, even frugal, streak."

In any case, merely a partial listing of the Queen's holdings would show a prodigious real estate portfolio, ranging from city property to Balmoral Castle on 50,000 acres in Scotland. There are also stocks, works of art, precious objects of many descriptions, and thoroughbred racehorses, in which the Queen has shown a keen and abiding interest. Much of her wealth has been passed down to her. Nevertheless, as *Fortune* put it pithily: "Her pragmatic Majesty has invested wisely."

Above: Queen Elizabeth II and her Private Secretary, Sir William Heseltine, at the races on Derby day at Epsom, in 1989. Left: Queen Elizabeth II taking the salute from the Ivory Phaeton Coach at the 1989 Trooping the Colour ceremony marking her official birthday.

BEATRIX

QUEEN OF THE NETHERLANDS

Like quite a few other monarchs these days, Beatrix, Queen of the Netherlands since 1980, spends much of her time balancing centuries of tradition with a practical approach to modern life. Polls consistently show that the Dutch public approves of the results. As historian Coenraad Tamse of Groningen University put it, the royal family "belongs to the antique furniture that we've inherited, and it would be unwise to do away with it – they might be very valuable."

Along with the antiques, Beatrix and her family preside over a portfolio of assets that includes jewelry, corporate stocks and an estate in the Hague where they make their home. Estimates of their net worth vary widely; at the upper end of the range, Fortune magazine has put it at $4.4 billion.

Although the queen is far from a figurehead, her official statements are closely tailored to fit the policy of the elected government. An attractive woman with the characteristic rosy cheeks of her people, Beatrix usually appears in public dressed like a

Below: Queen Beatrix and Prince Claus with Queen Elizabeth II and the Duke of Edinburgh before a state banquet at Buckingham Palace in 1982.

prosperous middle-class matron. Except for on state occasions, she is driven around in a Ford.

She and her husband, Claus, a former West German diplomat, eschew extravagance. Their three sons study in the state-run university system and room with friends. But Beatrix reportedly is concerned with maintaining respect for the monarchy and insists on being called "your Majesty," rather than "Ma'am", which her mother Juliana preferred.

Over the centuries, her family – the House of Orange – has survived

Facing page top: Queen Beatrix at a farewell ceremony at the Schiphol airport after a state visit by President Bush in 1989. Facing page bottom: the royal family posing in the garden of their Huis ten Bosch (Garden in the Woods) Palace in the Hague in 1983: (left to right) Prince Johan-Frisco, Queen Beatrix, Prince Willem-Alexander, Prince Claus and Prince Constantijn.

Left: Queen Beatrix salutes the Queen's Flag at the Palace Noordeinde on Prinsjedag (Little Prince's Day), which marks the official opening of the Dutch parliamentary year. Below left: Queen Beatrix, accompanied by (left) her husband, Prince Claus, and (right) her son, Prince Willem-Alexander, arriving to give her annual speech at the opening of the Dutch Parliament in 1989.

financial and romantic scandal, as well as the occupation of the realm by Napoleon's forces in 1795-1812 and by Hitler's in 1940-45.

The latest time of turbulence came when Juliana abdicated in favor of her daughter. During Beatrix's inauguration (Dutch monarchs are not crowned), stone-throwing squatters rioted outside. "In hindsight," said one longtime observer of the family's affairs, "the inauguration riots had less to do with the monarchy than with anything else – the housing situation, unemployment and the like. But as national symbols, the royals bore the brunt of the unrest."

CHAPTER 2

Sir James Goldsmith

In both his appearance and his style of doing business, this Anglo-French industrialist might have been the creation of a fictional movie scriptwriter. Six feet three inches tall, a fast-talking cigar smoker almost never seen without a tropical tan, he has been described as an almost equal blend of charmer and bully – a smiling, courtly shark. In a career of building, buying and selling businesses on both sides of the Atlantic from his base in London, "Sir Jimmy" has accumulated a nest egg estimated by *Fortune* magazine to be worth $1.4 billion. *Forbes*, on the other hand, declined to certify him as a billionaire, acknowledging his imposing financial assets, but wondering "how much debt did he have?"

Goldsmith started out with a pharmaceutical business in France in the 1950s, and then established Cavenham Foods in England, which he expanded

Above: a newly-married Goldsmith with his bride, Isabel Patine, then eighteen, the daughter of a Brazilian tin magnate. Left: Goldsmith at Buckingham Palace, where he received a knighthood from the Queen in 1976.

British financier Sir James Goldsmith in 1986.

until it ranked as one of Europe's biggest grocery conglomerates.

In time he disposed of Cavenham while putting together an elaborate international network of other ventures, much of it anchored in the tax-favorable ground of the Cayman Islands. At one of his properties, the French magazine *L'Express*, he exerted a typically mercurial presence. In the assessment of a *L'Express* editor whom Goldsmith fired after a political disagreement, "He's an English eccentric in the best sense of the term. He is sometimes downright reactionary, but he is also fiercely anti-Establishment, left, right and center."

On the eve of the 1980s, Goldsmith loudly bemoaned what he described as a lack of promising business opportunities in England. He turned his attention to the United States in plenty of time to become a major figure among the American "corporate raiders" at the height of the Wall Street boom. Some observers are betting he will be back in the '90s making waves in the British Isles.

"I prefer making money to spending it."
That was the credo Harry Helmsley
avowed *en route* from a modest
childhood as the son of a dry goods
salesman to building a real estate
empire embracing hotels, commercial
properties such as a part interest in New
York's Empire State Building, and
enough apartment buildings to house
50,000 families. But somehow the
philosophy seemed to change after
Helmsley broke off a marriage of thirty
three years to wed Leona Roberts, a onetime cigarette girl turned real estate
broker, in 1972.

For a while they seemed to
complement each other handsomely.
The mustachioed, bespectacled Harry,
who had adopted the Quaker faith years
earlier, stuck to his role as behind-the-

Above: Harry and Leona
Helmsley during a 1985
news conference
announcing that the
Harley of New York was
to be officially changed to
the New York Helmsley
Hotel. Facing page left:
Harry and Leona
Helmsley posing under a
giant top hat atop the
then Harley of New York
Hotel in 1980. Facing
page right: the Helmsleys
at their Helmsley Palace
Hotel, which boasts: "It's
the only palace in the
world where the queen
stands guard."

scenes dealer and investor, maintaining and adding to their $1.5 billion-plus fortune. Leona, by contrast, assumed the mantle of "queen" of the Helmsley hotels, featuring herself in a high-visibility advertising campaign. She also embarked on an elaborate renovation of their palatial home in the New York suburb of Greenwich, Connecticut.

Then the government accused the Helmsleys of avoiding taxes by accounting for personal purchases, ranging from a marble dance floor to a few pairs of underwear, as businesses expenses. Harry, by then eighty years old and ailing, was pronounced incapable of standing trial. That left Leona, sixty-nine, to face her accusers in the summer of 1989 amid a sea of news cameras, microphones and reporters from around the world. In testimony, Leona was portrayed as a cold, abrasive social climber who had once asserted that "only the little people pay taxes."

Mrs. Helmsley and her lawyers protested that this portrait was unfair.

Perhaps she was unpopular with her employees, they conceded, but how could a couple who had paid $57.8 million in taxes over a span of three years be described as disdaining their rightful obligations? Their pleas were made in vain.

Leona was found guilty of tax evasion. In the court of public opinion, at the same time, it appeared she had been given an irreversible conviction for the offenses of arrogance and greed.

Leona and Harry Helmsley surrounded by the media in 1989.

AHMED JUFFALI

You didn't have to be an oil sheikh to get rich from the sudden wave of prosperity that swept into the Middle East in the years since World War II. The money that oil brought created demand for many other things - construction, industrialization and consumer products. Juffali and his two brothers were in the right place, at the right time, with the right contacts, to meet many of those needs and wants - and amass a billion-dollar fortune along the way.

E.A. Juffali & Brothers, in recent years the largest private business in Saudi Arabia apart from banks, started out on a modest scale. It built electric power systems for small towns and settlements being formed by Saudis who were succumbing to the blandishments of such things as air-conditioning. As the story is told, the Saudi royal family liked the results of the Juffalis' work, and favored the company when the construction projects to be done became bigger and more numerous. When it faced challenges too big to tackle on its own, the Juffali firm made extensive use of foreign partners.

Meanwhile, the family was also on the alert to capitalize on a burgeoning consumer market for modern products and luxury goods. For instance, it secured the franchise to distribute Mercedes-Benz automobiles in Saudi Arabia. Among the other international giants with whom they lined up business arrangements were Siemens, International Business Machines and Michelin.

The Saudis' pace of spending and investment slowed in the mid- to late-1980s as the oil boom cooled off. Nevertheless, ample opportunities still seemed likely for the Juffali brothers in a nation working hard to prepare itself for the twenty-first century.

DONALD TRUMP

In the early weeks of the 1990s, historic change was in the air. Communist governments tottered or collapsed. Much of Europe hurtled rapidly toward a new economic order. The Cold War that had dominated global politics for nearly half a century seemed to have come to a sudden and unexpected end. But in many of the world's newspapers and broadcasts, these stories were shouldered aside by another cosmic development: Donald J. Trump of New York City wanted to divorce his wife, Ivana.

To many observers, this hullabaloo

was an outrageous case of misplaced priorities. Yet others saw it as a telling commentary on the temper of the times. For if there was one single living, breathing symbol of success and excess anywhere, it was Trump. When this man buys – something which happens often – he seldom stops at just taking title. He also puts his name on it, whether it is a Manhattan real estate project, an Atlantic City casino, or an airline. In his spare time he has come forth with Trump the Board game, the Tour de Trump bicycle race, and even the bestselling book *Trump: The Art of the*

Donald Trump (above) with his wife Ivana, after she was shown in as a U.S. citizen in 1988, and (left) with New York City Parks Commissioner Henry Stern, lifting cement to begin the rebuilding in 1986 of the Wolman skating rink in Central Park. Trump financed the project.

Left: Trump poses with one of the three Sikorsky helicopters of Trump Air, a helicopter service from New York to his Atlantic City casinos. Below left: Donald Trump with his father Fred Trump (left) and boxing promoter Don King.

Facing page top: Trump's yacht, the 300-foot-long *Trump Princess*. He bought it for $30 million and spent another $10 million on refitting. In 1988 he invited Miss America contestants (facing page bottom) onto the yacht in Atlantic City, New Jersey, for a photo session .

Deal. He has been satirized in comic strips, vilified as an egomaniac, and extolled as a promotional genius. No one has yet accused him, however, of being out of step with the times.

"I don't do it for the money," he declared at the start of his book. "I do it to do it. Deals are my art form."

Even so, if it is truly the game that inspires him, he still seems acutely aware of the score. After the stock market crash in 1987, he quickly advised reporters that he had sold before the bottom dropped out. He has estimated his wealth at close to $5 billion, while arbiters like *Forbes* and *Fortune* magazines put it closer to $1.5 billion.

Above left: Trump inspects Williamsburg Bridge in New York with Alfred Dellibovi, head of the US Urban Mass Transportation Administration. Trump put up an estimated $250 million to rehabilitate the deteriorating structure. Left: announcing "Wrestlemania IV" at the Trump Plaza in Atlantic City, Donald Trump holds high the World Wrestling Federation championship belt. He is flanked by wrestlers Hulk Hogan (left) and Andre the Giant.

Even within his carefully crafted public image, there are striking contrasts. Millions not lavished on his ostentatious yacht go to causes like AIDS research. For a self-proclaimed believer in taking the offensive, he spends a lot of time defending himself. "One of the problems when you become successful is that jealously and envy inevitably follow," he has said. "There are people – I categorize them as life's losers – who get their sense of accomplishment and achievement from trying to stop others. As far as I'm concerned, if they had any real ability they wouldn't be fighting me, they'd be doing something constructive themselves."

Whatever its source, Trump appears to be possessed of inexhaustible energy. While other business barons of the 1980s succumbed to scandal or simply wore themselves out, he showed no sign of running out of steam.

"It is difficult to imagine that Donald Trump could ever walk away from center ring in the real estate world," said Jerome Tuccille at the conclusion of his 1985 book entitled – what else? – *Trump*. "Wherever the action is, and whatever form it takes, one suspects he will be in the middle of it. He cannot help himself. He has everything, and yet one suspects he is driven to do more."

Above: Trump and British entertainer Benny Hill showing off the Benny Hill salute in front of the Trump Tower in New York. Left: Trump with middleweight champion Thomas Hearns (left) and challenger Michael Olajide announcing a title bout at the Trump Taj Mahal Casino Resort.

RONALD PERELMAN

There doesn't ever seem to have been any doubt that Ronald Perelman was destined for a business career. As a schoolboy in the 1950s he was attending board meetings of his father's Philadelphia company, and he is said to have become an expert reader of accounting statements before he was old enough to start business school. Still, he has surprised even those familiar with his precocious reputation in some of the biggest deals he has pulled off, most notably the $3 billion takeover of the international cosmetics giant Revlon in 1986.

Revlon became the crown jewel of a collection of businesses with very little in common - candy, cigars, camping equipment, health testing laboratories and a savings and loan, among others. Rather than a feel for any given business, Perelman has relied on a flair for buying stagnant or troubled ventures at bargain prices using borrowed money. Once he has bought a company, he is renowned for moving rapidly to cut costs, sell assets and realize profits to create a steppingstone towards a bigger future deal.

It's generally agreed that Perelman has achieved billionaire status. But precise fixes on his net worth have been hard to obtain, in part because of his heavy use of debt financing. *Fortune* magazine put his wealth at $3.2 billion; *Forbes* would say only that it "may be over $1 billion." Though he looks to have many years of dealing still ahead, it remains to be seen how and whether he will adapt his style to the new debt-wary climate that prevailed in the business world as the 1990s began.

Abrasive and hard-charging in the daytime world, Perelman for some years was known to prefer retiring to bed not much later than his four children. With his second marriage in the mid-1980s, however, he started to be seen more often at nighttime social gatherings.

FRIEDRICH KARL FLICK

Start with tales of romance and intrigue in an opulent villa where the business baron lives with a onetime chambermaid. Add a whiff of political scandal, and stir in generous amounts of internecine battling over control of the family fortune.

It might well be the recipe for prime-time television soap opera. But in this instance it is the nonfictional story of the life and times of this Munich tycoon.

Flick cashed in a good many of his business chips in 1985 when he sold his industrial empire to the mighty Deutsche Bank for something in the neighborhood of $3 billion. He retained his standing, however, as a major force in the power structure of European finance with a seat on Deutsche Bank's supervisory board and large insurance-company interests, as well as by dint of his sheer wealth alone.

Events, meanwhile, were conspiring to leave him little time to rest on his laurels. Having ridden out a storm of controversy in the early 1980s over political contributions, he now was faced with a legal challenge from two nephews laying claim to some of the family assets. The dispute was apparently resolved, with Flick agreeing to pay his relatives a sum that wasn't disclosed.

Rumours regularly circulate about what his next business move might be. Whatever comes along, he seems to be prepared. The Munich retreat he shares with his companion, Ingrid Rugger, has a staff of more than one hundred and includes a shelter designed to withstand an atomic-bomb attack.

German industrialist
Friedrich Karl Flick.

EDMOND SAFRA

The description "international banker" fits Edmond Safra like a perfectly tailored suit. A Brazilian citizen raised in Lebanon and now living in Switzerland, he has banking and other financial interests stretching from Tokyo through North and South America and Europe to Beirut. While he is frequently described as secretive or mysterious, one thing is known for certain – he is persistent.

After starting one big enterprise, known as the Trade Development Bank, in the 1960s, he sold it to the U.S.-based financial services conglomerate American Express in 1984 for more than half a billion dollars in securities, and assumed a senior title at American Express. The relationship did not go smoothly, however, and the two went their separate ways. As soon as a contractual agreement between the parties permitted, Safra started a new banking venture on the same Geneva street where Amex had its local office.

Along about this time, some people at American Express evidently said some not-so-nice things about Safra that soon reached his ears, and he threatened to take his former colleagues to court. A settlement was reached in which American Express paid either $4 million or $8 million, depending on who's account you choose to believe. The new bank, Safra Republic, is financially allied with the Republic National Bank of New York, which in turn counts Edmond Safra as a major stockholder.

He has two brothers who run a prosperous private bank in Brazil. Safra's wife, also Brazilian, inherited a big appliance business from a previous marriage. All told, the family assets are estimated $1.5 billion to $2 billion, with perhaps not every penny counted.

This silver-haired patriarch of a billionaire Italian family got a rolling start toward a life of wealth – from a grandfather who joined up with some associates in 1899 to form an enterprise called Fabbrica Italiana Automobili Torino. Today the initials of that name still spell Fiat, the imprint on more than half the cars sold in Italy and about one in every seven throughout Europe.

But nobody has ever accused Agnelli – known to intimates as Gianni and to the public press as *l'Avvocato*, the Lawyer – of just clipping coupons and

Above left: Giovanni and Marella Agnelli, among the bluebloods of Italy attending the premiere of *Tevere Blu* in Rome in 1954. Left: the Fiat Mirafiori car assembly lines in Turin.

Left: Giovanni Agnelli with his wife, Marella, in 1983, and (below) the final assembly line of the Fiat auto plant in Cassino.

Agnelli owns sumptuous homes in New York and St. Moritz, as well as an estate outside his native Turin. Among his other pursuits, he sits on the board of directors of Italy's most influential investment bank. Said a rival more recently arrived in the ranks of Italy's super-rich: "I never forget that he's the emperor."

coasting along. When people coined terms like "industrialist" and "power broker," they surely had somebody very much like Agnelli in mind.

At the time of this writing, Fiat Auto still brought in more than half the profits of the family business, which had revenues in 1988 of $34 billion. Other ventures, however, had taken it into engineering and construction, insurance, food, retailing, publishing and a wide range of additional businesses. Observers saw this as a shrewd response to the threat of increased competition in auto manufacturing from the Japanese. Like other business leaders around Europe, Agnelli was also faced with the challenge of preparing for the dismantling of trade barriers set to take effect in 1992 within the European Common Market. That landmark event is expected to diminish many an old commercial fortune, and help create more than a few new ones. To further the company's international prospects, in the late 1980s Fiat gained listing for its publicly traded shares on the New York Stock Exchange.

Agnelli in 1990.

THE REICHMANN BROTHERS

Battery Park, New York.

How far can you go in real estate? That would be a good question to put to the brothers Reichmann – Albert, Paul and Ralph – whose $8-billion-plus empire ranks them indisputably among the richest families anywhere on earth. At the beginning of the 1990s they owned more commercial property in New York City than anybody else, including Battery Park City at the southern tip of Manhattan. They had office buildings in Toronto, Ottawa, Los Angeles, Chicago and Boston. They were spending more than $5 billion to develop the huge

Canary Wharf complex in London's East End, which was scheduled to include the tallest building in that city. In their spare time, there was a $65-million civic center to be built in Jerusalem. And just to diversify things a bit, there was a portfolio of corporate stockholdings with a market value that approached $5 billion.

Though such resources might entitle anybody to enjoy a lavish life style, the Reichmanns think otherwise. They are strict Orthodox Jews whose austere dress and aversion to self-promotion sets them far apart from a good many of their compatriots. When their names do get into the news, it is most often for something such as Albert's leading role in raising money for Armenian victims of the devastating earthquake of December 1988.

When the brothers were young, the whole family fled its native Europe to escape the advancing Nazis. In the 1950s they reached Canada and began a business that concentrated first on trading and exporting commodities such as steel. Then the real estate development projects, and their wealth, started going up. Modest as they were in their demeanor, the Reichmanns and their Olympia & York real estate company acquired a reputation for shrewdness, daring and, above all, thinking big.

In recent years that image of near-infallibility has faced some stern challenges. It became clear that Canary Wharf in London was an undertaking fraught with risk. The Reichmanns also became entangled, through loans and stock investments, in an ill-fated venture with a fellow Canadian, Robert Campeau, involving retailing in the United States. At the height of the Christmas shopping season in 1989, such tiny U.S. retailers as Bloomingdale's, Jordan Marsh and Lazarus made headlines not for the merchandise they were moving but for the debts they could not pay.

As big a story as that might have been, however, it represented only one piece of a jigsaw puzzle the Reichmanns had put together around the world. And, said *Fortune* magazine, "If the Reichmanns have erred in linking up with Campeau, it will have been a rare misstep for them."

COSTAS MICHAEL LEMOS

A sense of timing can be a formidable asset when you are trying to make a billion-dollar fortune, or to protect your wealth once you have amassed it. For a case study in the art of knowing when to play and when to walk away, consider Costas Lemos – a man who, in a world of Onassises and Niarchoses, has frequently been described as the richest Greek shipping magnate of them all.

Trained in the law, Lemos went to work as a captain in merchant shipping and began to build up his own fleet after World War II. During the 1960s his ships were worth more than those of any of his fabled rivals from his native land. But, apparently sensing a change in the economic tide that would depress cargo rates and the value of his vessels, he sold off many of them in exchange for cash and real estate.

By the late 1980s, as he approached his eightieth birthday, Lemos was said to have parked more than two-thirds of an estimated $3.5 billion nest egg in cash and readily marketable securities.

Another 20% was invested in real estate, most notably in the United States, but also in his adoptive home of Switzerland and in London as well as in Greece. Not much more than 10% of his wealth was still committed to the shipping business.

Forbes magazine declined to confer its formal stamp of billionaire status on Lemos, saying his secretive ways made pinning down the value of his holdings too elusive a task. Whatever the extent of his wealth, it has a designated heir in son Michael Costas. Lemos also has two daughters, Chrysanthi and Irini.

This billionaire businessman is a Saudi Arabian native with distinctly Western tastes. He married an American, wears American suits, and invests a lot of his money on Wall Street. As of the late 1980s, his direct and indirect shareholdings in U.S. companies included Occidental Petroleum, the conglomerate Transamerica, and the bank holding companies Chase Manhattan, First Chicago, and J.P. Morgan & Company.

Olayan, in his early seventies, was just four when his father, a spice merchant in the city of Medina, died. He studied at the American Mission School in Bahrain, then worked in the oil industry before starting a construction company with the help of a $4,000 loan. As he branched out into banking and other types of financing deals over the years, the numbers involved in his transactions grew correspondingly. In 1988, when the New York investment firm of First Boston joined its European affiliate, Credit Suisse First Boston, in a $1.1 billion merger, $600 million of short-term financing was provided by an outfit called SSO Ltd, stamping the loan with the clear imprint of Olayan's initials.

Within the confines of his native land, Olayan is a top executive and investor in the Saudi British Bank, which has assets of nearly $3 billion. In its more recent estimate, *Forbes* magazine pegged his personal net worth at $1 billion plus.

Chapter 3

Media

JOHN KLUGE

For most of his seventy-five-plus years John Kluge (pronounced Clue-gi) has been performing impressive tricks with money and businesses. He transformed himself from an impoverished German immigrant who went to college on scholarship into one of the richest private financiers in the United States. It was not just for what he achieved, but how he achieved it, that the business press has dubbed him "the magician" and "the master of creative finance." *Forbes* recently ranked him as America's richest man.

The primary vehicle for his exploits has been Metromedia Incorporated, whose predecessor company was a modest, struggling broadcasting business when Kluge first invested in it in the 1950s. In the years that followed he transformed Metromedia's financial structure several times through purchases and sales of assets, exchanges of stock for borrowed money and borrowed money for stock, and other manoeuvres. By one estimate, he parlayed an initial $8 million stake into $1.5 billion over the span of about twenty years.

In other situations Kluge has showed a deft hand at the first and simplest rule of wealth-building – buy low and sell high. When the cellular telephone business boomed in the late 1980s, he owned choice territories in the northeastern United States that tripled

Above: John Kluge (right) with Malcolm Forbes, Elizabeth Taylor and Patricia Kluge at Forbes' 1989 birthday bash in Morocco.

Facing page: John and Patricia Kluge greeting Virginia Governor L. Douglas Wilder at a reception in 1990. Kluge was a major contributor to the governor's campaign fund.

in value to about $2.6 billion. Other properties in which he holds or has held an interest include Orion Pictures in the movie business; the Ponderosa chain of family restaurants; the Harlem Globetrotters basketball team, and the Ice Capades traveling ice show. His current net worth has been pegged at least $5 billion.

With that kind of cushion to rest on, Kluge may attempt less derring-do in the 1990s than he has in the past. In any case, the feats he has already pulled off will be studied by newcomers to the world of investment banking for years to come.

Above: Metromedia president John Kluge (left) with Los Angeles Mayor Tom Bradley and entertainer Frank Sinatra at a Hollywood salute to the city's bicentennial in 1981.

Right: John and Patricia Kluge with other celebrities at New York's Carnegie Hall for a benefit concert for the World Mercy Fund given by Frank Sinatra.

Barbara Cox Anthony and Anne Cox Chambers

James Cox (left), former governor and publisher, with running mate Franklin D. Roosevelt in Dayton, Ohio, 1920.

These sisters, children of the 1920s, own a newspaper and broadcasting empire that qualifies them for widespread recognition as the wealthiest women in the United States. Their combined net worth is perhaps $5 billion or even more.

The business, Cox Enterprises, came into being just before the turn of the century when Barbara and Anne's father, James Middleton Cox, paid $26,000 to buy a daily newspaper in Dayton, Ohio. James, who had earlier worked as a country schoolteacher and newspaper reporter, was elected to the U.S. House of Representatives before he reached the age of forty, and subsequently served as governor of Ohio. In 1920, he was the unsuccessful nominee of the Democratic Party for the presidency of the United States, heading a ticket that carried the name of Franklin D. Roosevelt for vice president.

Following this disappointment, Cox went back to nurturing his communications business until his death in 1957. Today the business includes daily and weekly newspapers, radio and TV stations, cable TV properties, even an auto auction enterprise.

Anne Cox Chambers in
the 1970s.

Elder daughter Anne, a divorced mother of three, was once the ambassador to Belgium and is now a civic leader in Atlanta, Georgia. She also maintains luxurious residences in New York and Provence. Barbara, a resident of Honolulu, owns cattle ranches in the United States and Australia. Her son James Cox Kennedy, in his early forties, became chairman of Cox Enterprises in 1988.

Chairman of the board of the *Atlanta Constitution* newspaper, Ann Cox Chambers campaigns for Jimmy Carter in 1976.

TED TURNER

In a buttoned-down business world of computerized calculations, Ted Turner has proved there is still a place for the brash adventurer. Not all of the high-risk missions on which he has embarked from his home base of Atlanta, Georgia, have succeeded, and he has accumulated his share of enemies and detractors along the way. But nobody questions the scope of his imagination or his willingness to try, and often achieve, things that others said couldn't, or shouldn't, be done.

The highlights of his improbable life include being the pioneer of the TBS cable television "superstation" and the CNN national all-news TV channel; the yachtsman whose crew won the 1977 America's Cup with *Courageous*; an owner of professional baseball and basketball teams and the originator of the Goodwill Games, an international sports competition, and the colorizer of classic black-and-white films despite the protests of legions of movie buffs. The twice-divorced father of five, he is known by the sobriquets "Captain Outrageous" and "the Mouth of the South."

Turner launched his business career in the 1960s by injecting new life into an advertising-billboard company he inherited from his father. He put the billboards to further use promoting radio stations he acquired, and later turned a local TV outlet into a national medium (WTBS, for Turner Broadcasting System) through the then-

Above: Ted Turner, temporarily manager of his Atlanta Braves baseball team.

Facing page: Ted Turner, skipper of *Courageous*, winner of the 1977 America's Cup.

fledgling means of cable and satellite transmission.

In the mid-1980s he bid unsuccessfully for control of one of America's prime entertainment properties, CBS, then captured a separate billion-dollar prize when he bought MGM's film library (which provided his entrée into the "colorizing" game using a new high-tech process). Debt problems threatened to sink him for a time, but with the financial aid of cable TV operators he was soon back on course. A runup in the price of Turner Broadcasting stock helped propel his personal net worth well past $1 billion in the late 1980s. Barely past the age of fifty as a new decade began, Turner seemed a likely prospect to be a big player in the story of the 1990s as well.

Above: Ted Turner getting help from his son Rhett, then eleven, sanding the boom of *Courageous*.

Right: Turner on the afterdeck of his twenty-one-meter yacht *Courageous*.

Turner outside the Atlanta studios of his CNN.

Ted Turner in the newsroom of his Cable News Network.

Kerry Packer displays his passion for polo – even on his hat.

Befitting their country's high-spirited image, wealthy Australians who attract world attention tend to be young, adventurous types. In several cases, their stars have fallen as quickly as they rose. Still, one individual stands in this volatile environment as an acknowledged billionaire – Kerry Packer, publishing magnate, industrialist and world-scale wheeler and dealer.

There is no mistaking Packer for the diffident, coupon-clipping sort. True, he got his start with the help of an inheritance from his father, known to be a stern task-master, who died in 1974. Like a good many other tycoons portrayed in this book, however, Packer proved his hand by making a small fortune into a big one.

For instance, through growth and acquisitions he has captured an estimated two-thirds of the Australian market for magazines at Consolidated Press Holdings, of which he is chairman. He invested something in the order of half a billion dollars to buy a dominant position in Australian National Industries, a diversified engineering company. He has dealt or made bids in such British businesses as Courtauld's and BAT Industries. In still other ventures he has shown a predilection for both the city – office buildings in Perth and Melbourne – and the country – sprawling cattle stations in Queensland and the Northern Territory.

Packer's spare-time passion for polo playing attests to his appetite for high style and risk-taking. In his business dealings, a generous measure of practicality tempers his flair for the dramatic. As one of his associates told *Forbes* magazine: "We buy based on a company's track record and not on its future blue sky."

Publishing entrepreneur Robert Maxwell gives the thumbs-up as the first edition of his *London Daily News* (right) rolled off the press in February 1987. The newspaper competed with the *London Standard*, then the only afternoon paper in London.

Maxwell dressed in traditional Moroccan costume (below) for the 70th birthday party of Malcolm Forbes (center) in Tangier. Maxwell's wife is at right.

"Child of Czech Peasants Becomes Fleet Street Tycoon!" With such a headline might one of Ian Robert Maxwell's newspapers begin to tell his rags-to-riches tale. But success and a fortune worth $1.5 billion or more haven't rubbed off all his rough edges. Indeed, he seems as proud of his maverick image as he is of anything he has accomplished. "I have always been an outsider," he once said in an interview with U.S. News & World Report. "In fact, I fear that I am in danger of becoming a member of the Establishment."

Traditionalists who are offended by Maxwell's brash, mercurial style might vow that he need not worry on that score. Even among his critics, however, he has won admiration for his energy, his business acumen and his resilience in the face of adversity. Said one more conventional English industrialist, "If we had ten men like Robert Maxwell, Britain would not have suffered from

Robert Maxwell in 1988.

Maxwell and British actor
Rupert Everett cut the
ribbon to open the British
Pavilion at the Cannes
Film Festival in 1987.

the economic problems that have plagued it since the war."

Maxwell, now in his late sixties, was born Jan Ludwig Hoch, the only son in a large Czechoslovakian farm family. Today he controls such far flung assets as the Mirror Group Newspapers; television investments in England, France, Spain and Macao; Macmillan Publishing, and an airline-guide business he bought from Dun & Bradstreet of the United States. In 1990, Maxwell attained another of his long-held aims: the successful launch of *The European*, an English-language newspaper circulating throughout Europe.

Though he has had his share of run-ins with other members of the press, Maxwell seems to thrive on public attention – to the extent of retaining a personal photographer. Sometimes he is caricatured as a beetle-browed knight errant, forever stirring up controversy. Other, less irreverent, portraits depict him as a nonstop workaholic juggling multiple business appointments by telephone from his helicopter as it ferries him from his home in Oxford to his London office.

Ever the champion of the underdog, he has taken prominent roles in efforts to alleviate famine in Ethiopia and to build the "Chunnel" under the English Channel connecting Britain with Continental Europe.

Maxwell holding up a copy of the *Daily Mirror* (below) as he announces that he has bought the Daily Mirror Newspaper Group – consisting of the *Daily Mirror*, the *Sunday Mirror*, the *Sunday People*, the *Sporting Life* and two Scottish newspapers, the *Daily Record* and the *Sunday Mail* – for $147.42 million (113.4 million pounds).

SILVIO BERLUSCONI

Above: Sylvio Berlusconi, Italian TV network magnate and chairman of France's Fight TV network, in 1986.

Though the world may have its share of shy, reclusive billionaires, this broadcasting baron from Italy will never fit that description. He brought in some of his first paychecks singing popular songs and playing dance dates in a band with friends. Today visitors to his home in Milan, a one-time monastery, may wind up dancing in the downstairs disco or listening to Silvio at the piano, still singing his heart out.

By all accounts, Berlusconi the entertainer works every bit as hard as he plays. A decade ago he started the first private television network in Italy,

Facing page top: Berlusconi, flanked on the left by Christophe Riboud and on the right by Jerome Seydoux, presenting their new TV channel, France's fifth, in 1985.

Facing page bottom: Berlusconi and Italian film director Franco Zeffirelli announcing their collaboration in 1987 on a super-production about the French Revolution.

which soon helped propel him to success when a court ruled that the government could not maintain its TV monopoly. Today his three Italian channels beam out their signals for eighteen hours a day, and he has expanded into French and West German television as well. And where might one go to buy time for a commercial message on a Berlusconi-broadcast program? You might try Publitalia, his advertising agency.

A more recent investment, made in the name of diversification, was the $650 million purchase of a majority interest in the La Standa department store chain. He has yet another winner in his Milan A.C. soccer team.

When he is not singing, Berlusconi is perfectly willing to speak up for himself. He has claimed to possess far more wealth, most of it unencumbered by the claims of any partners or family members, than the $2.8 billion estimated by *Fortune* magazine. Since he is still in his mid-fifties, he has plenty of time to shoot for even bigger things. One bet he has been making of late: pay TV.

CHAPTER 4

FAMILY

Left: L'Oreal's "Anais Anais" perfume.

Bottom: part of Nestlé's range of chocolate-based products.

about $400 million – roughly half the value of the piece of L'Oreal she gave up. A costly mistake? Not necessarily. After all, while most of us seek ways to get money, the billionaire faces a very different and daunting challenge – keeping it. That means protecting it from the virulent forces of taxation and inflation, competition and change. In Bettencourt's case, diversification meant spreading her risks beyond the fickle tastes of the cosmetics customer. It's the kind of proposition many a wealthy person would instantly embrace – exchanging a substantial portion of one's assets for the greater assurance of keeping the rest.

She's generally considered the richest individual in France – and what better credentials could anyone have for such a position than the stewardship of a cosmetics and fragrance empire? Bettencourt's father, Eugene Schuller, put a genius for chemistry to work founding L'Oreal, at last reckoning still the biggest company in a business that has fostered several of the world's largest family fortunes. If the idea of a nest egg worth something like $1.5 billion seems remote to you, consider that you helped to create and sustain it if you have ever bought such brand names as Anais Anais, Lancome or Preference. In the late 1980s, L'Oreal's worldwide sales exceeded $4.5 billion a year.

The business may be flamboyant, but Bettencourt favors a subdued style of living with husband Andre, a onetime government minister, in a Parisian suburb. She once owned about half of L'Oreal, before deciding to diversify by swapping part of that stake for a chunk of Nestle, the Swiss-based global food conglomerate, in the mid-1970s.

Over the next decade and a half, reckons *Forbes* magazine, that move cost her a fair amount of money. As of mid-1989, her Nestle investment was worth

Al-Rajhi and his brothers, who live in the Saudi Arabian capital of Riyadh, made a big chunk of their $2 billion-plus fortune in ARABIC – an acronym for Al-Rajhi Banking & Investment Corporation, the modern descendant of a decades-old money-changing business. As of mid-1989, their 52% stake in the bank had a market value of more than $600 million. Their separate assets, invested in real estate and a variety of businesses, were said to be worth at least twice that amount.

For many years the Al-Rajhis technically weren't bankers at all. They took "deposits" from their customers for such purposes as temporary safekeeping or payment of international transactions. But most of those customers, being devout Moslems, were governed by the Koran's proscription against accepting interest on a loan, no matter what the going market rate. Thus the Al-Rajhis had access to the funds at virtually no cost.

While it was in their hands, they were free to invest the "float" wherever they saw an opportunity. At the peak of the oil boom, in the 1970s and early 1980s, this continuous pool of operating funds is reported to have reached totals exceeding $4 billion. The family put it to work in things like agricultural projects and real estate, both in Saudi Arabia and elsewhere around the world. Among their holdings at last report were some properties in Washington, D.C.

As modern times and Western ways crept increasingly into Saudi life, they acceded to pressures from the powers that be to become a banking operation of the more standard kind. While that may have cramped their former style, it by no means put them out of business. Indeed, the Al-Rajhis showed their adaptability to changing times with a highly successful offering of ARABIC stock in 1988 to the new breed of Saudi investor.

JOHANNA QUANDT

It seems only fitting that a popular badge of affluence in many corners of the world, the BMW automobile, should itself be the foundation of one of the world's great family fortunes. Johanna Quandt, in her late sixties, is the widow of one of two half-brothers who invested in the West German car manufacturer when it was struggling through hard times in the 1950s. Today the family owns a majority interest in the company with a value that has been estimated at more than $2.5 billion.

A long-standing rumor has it that the Quandts want to sell out. So far there has been nothing to substantiate that speculation. But even if the Quandts were forced by some unlikely circumstance to unload at a distress price, they would not exactly be candidates for the poorhouse. There is a

BMW presented this 503 car at the International Automobile Exhibition in Frankfurt in 1955.

Left: the BMW 1957 Isetta "Luxury Plus" model.

The distinctive BMW outward appearance, inner luxuriousness and quiet ride were all features of the BMW 535i (below) for the 1989 model year – at a $43,500 base price.

portfolio of other investments reported to include some one hundred stocks, and the family has made a recent foray into the credit card business, buying American Data Card Corporation of the U.S. for about $175 million.

The Quandt fortune traces its origins back through several generations to when the family engaged in such businesses as textiles and mining. Johanna may have acquired her position by legacy, but she is described as a savvy and active participant in business affairs. Under her supervision, BMW enjoyed a resurgence of profitability in the late 1980s with the introduction of new models that beat the competition from Mercedes-Benz in sales to European buyers.

BMWs, in this instance a 318iS, are sold under the tag "The Ultimate Driving Machine."

THE BASS FAMILY

Biosphere II, one of the most daunting environmental undertakings ever, nears completion in 1990.

When you run short of worlds to conquer, build a new one of your own. That seems to be the idea that struck Edward Bass, a third-generation member of a Texas family that parlayed a good-sized oil fortune into a much bigger empire playing the corporate takeover game in the 1980s.

Ed is spending an estimated $30 million to build an artificial living environment for plants, animals and people called Biosphere II on two and one half acres in the southwestern United States. Complete with miniature ocean, desert and rain forest, the glass-enclosed "ecosystem" is described as both a scientific and commercial experiment. Could such a manmade setting one day house creatures from earth on some other planet? Or might it be used to replace a natural environment here on this planet that had been despoiled by pollution or some other blight?

The $5 billion fortune that makes such ventures possible for the Bass family dates back to the 1930s when Sid Richardson, a bachelor uncle, struck what proved to be a vast oil field in West Texas. When Richardson died some twenty five years later, he left most of his estate to a foundation. But there was still room for a $10 million bequest to the four sons of his nephew and partner, Perry Bass. The family soon diversified beyond energy into television and other businesses.

Then, as the 1980s dawned, they cut themselves in at an early stage on the takeover and buyout boom sweeping the corporate world. Investments in companies such as Walt Disney and Texaco reaped huge increases in their net worth.

Biosphere II is not the only activity that has thrust the family into the non-financial headlines of late. Brother Sid figured heavily in the gossip columns when he split with Anne, his wife of more than twenty years, and married New York socialite Mercedes Kellogg. The divorce cost him a reported $200 million.

Newt Bass (below) telling a tractor driver where to clear the ground for the Apple Valley Hospital in California's Mojave Desert in 1955. Newt launched a real estate boom in the western section of the desert, which then bloomed with irrigated farms, suburban communities, industrial developments and military bases.
Facing page: the Disney-MGM Studios Theme Park in Florida.

THE DORRANCE FAMILY

John T. Dorrance, Jr.,
chairman of Campbell
Soup Company.

Vast fortunes that last for generations can arise from a single good idea. In the case of the Dorrance family, now living in handsome style at various addresses around the United States, the wellspring was grandfather John T. Dorrance Sr.'s plan to sell condensed soup in cans.

Just before the end of the nineteenth century, the elder Dorrance, a chemistry whiz, turned down an offer of a teaching position to take a low-paying job in his uncle's business, then known

as the Campbell Preserve Company. He turned out to have a flair for salesmanship and business innovation as well as food chemistry. By 1914 the company had been renamed Campbell Soup and he was its president At his death in 1930, he left in trust to his children all the stock in Campbell's, worth close to $150 million in an era when $150 million really was a lot of money.

Son John Jr., known as Jack, joined the company in 1946 and became

Bottles fill with Prego spaghetti sauce on the assembly line in the Camden, New Jersey, plant of Campbell Soup Company.

Campbell Soup stock opened at $42 a share when it was admitted to trading on the New York Stock Exchange in 1954. Philip West (left), vice president of the Exchange, points to the board as a Campbell director, John Dorrance Jr. (center), and Campbell president William B. Murphy look on.

Campbell soups as they changed labels on the popular product, from left, in 1943, 1987, and 1988.

John T. Dorrance, Sr., had the original idea of selling condensed soup in cans – an innovative move that helped make his family's fortune.

chairman in 1962. By then Campbell had sold stock to the public, but the Dorrance family kept a majority interest for itself. Under Jack, Campbell prospered as a producer not only of its original product but also of such other brands as Pepperidge Farm baked goods and Swanson frozen foods (which gave the world the TV dinner). When Jack died in 1989, *Fortune* magazine estimated the family's net worth at $2.2 billion.

As usually happens with family business fortunes, the Dorrance wealth is starting to show signs of thinning out as it spreads through the branches of a widening family tree. But the price of Campbell stock increased during 1989 on speculation that the third generation of Dorrances might want to find a buyer for the company to reinvest their money over a more diversified base.

PRINCE JOHANNES VON THURN UND TAXIS

Are the rich, as F. Scott FitzGerald declared, really different from you and me? Those who would like to believe so didn't have to look much further than Germany's jet-setter, Prince Johannes von Thurn und Taxis, and his princess Gloria. The prince, who died aged 64 in December 1990, was considered one of Europe's richest men. He died of complications resulting from a second heart transplant. Chroniclers of the couple's often outrageous comings and goings had variously dubbed them the "TNT twins," befitting their initials, and the "king and queen of kitsch." She was less than half his age. They played their parts to the hilt, in a whirlwind world of yachts, motorcycles, costume balls and private hunting preserves.

Conspicuous though their consumption may have been, the money came from pockets as old as they are deep. The Thurn und Taxis fortune, estimated at $2.5-3 billion, dates back centuries to the days when the family were the sole postmasters to the Hapsburg empire. Their forebears may or may not have included the Italian Renaissance poet Tasso. The prince once said he was descended from Genghis Khan, and his wife from Attila the Hun.

No matter how they frolicked, they did not fritter away the family assets. The family owns vast acreage in the Black Forest, a big private bank, a brewery, metals and electronic businesses, and other real estate holdings from Brazil to Canada. The family businesses are embarked on ambitious ventures of property development and providing financial services to the world's ultrawealthy elite. Let us not forget the antiques, the artworks, and the millions in the Swiss bank account.

The prince once said of his marriage: "We are fighting all the time." But, he added, "we have the children, and that is all that matters."

Prince Johannes von Thurn und Taxis and his young wife Maria Gloria on their wedding day in June 1980.

The prince at a February 1990 press conference in his Regensburg castle.

Since billionaires often achieve what others only dream of, they tend to be an optimistic bunch. Not so Antonio Ermirio de Moraes, whose family controls the largest privately-owned industrial empire in Brazil and a fortune worth some $1.5 billion. Though he was named businessman of the year for ten years running by his country's most prominent financial publication, Ermirio can be positively cranky about the state of political and economic affairs in Brazil.

Speaking to reporters in 1988, for example, he lamented the government's "inability to overcome the economic crisis" and advised his fellow citizens to prepare for the worst. Yet when it was suggested that Ermirio might help improve the subject of his laments by taking over the reins himself, he declined to become finance minister and ruled himself out as a candidate for president. He said he couldn't make a political position fit his ethical standards.

For all that, however, the business decisions that Ermirio and his family make for their company Industrias Votorantim suggest a strong underlying confidence in the future. In 1988, for example, they bought a paper company, ventured into the orange juice business and announced plans for an addition to the string of power plants they operate.

Furthermore, the family has a long history of succeeding in adversity. Votorantim got its start in 1918 when Antonio Pereira Ignacio, an immigrant shoemaker from Portugal, acquired a textile plant that came up for auction as the result of a bank failure.

KENNETH THOMSON

This Canadian baron of the publishing, communications, retailing and travel industries bears more than a passing resemblance to the American comic-book hero "Superman." On the public stage he has wheeled and dealed his way to a $6-7 billion fortune in more-powerful-than-a-locomotive style. In private, he is very much the mild-mannered "Clark Kent," down to his dark- framed glasses and conservative dress. A Baptist who never smokes and seldom drinks alcoholic beverages, he has been married to the same woman since 1956, eschews press agentry and answers his own telephone. All that leaves him plenty of resources to devote to his collection of more than one hundred and fifty paintings by the Dutch-Canadian artist Cornelius Krieghoff.

Lord Thomson – he inherited the British title from his father – is the majority owner of a media conglomerate in Britain and North America that operates almost two hundred

Lord Thomson, chairman of the Thomson Organization, with his wife, his son David and his father, photographed at Claridge's in London in 1964.

Lord Thomson (on the right) in front of St. Basil's Cathedral in Moscow in 1963.

Lord Thomson with his son David and his father in 1964.

newspapers. In assembling his publishing empire, he gathered together a wide range of titles – for example, big-city dailies such as the *Globe and Mail* in his home base of Toronto, numerous small-town weekly newspapers, and such specialized publications as the *American Banker* and *Jane's Fighting Ships*, the authoritative reference source on naval warfare.

He also controls Hudson's Bay Company, operator of more than four hundred department stores; a major chain of British travel agencies, and ventures in financial services and real estate. A package of investments in North Sea energy endeavors, started by his father in the early 1970s, was recently sold off to help finance newer acquisitions.

Lord Thomson has an heir apparent in his son David and, in his late sixties, few illusions of immortality. "If you get any high-falutin' ideas about how important you are," he once observed, "look at a few skeletons and you'll soon come down to earth."

ALAN, LORD SAINSBURY AND FAMILY

Commerce and the arts play equally prominent roles in the affairs of this British clan, whose wealth has been conservatively estimated at $3 billion.

On the cultural side, the family has provided the financial impetus for an extension of the National Gallery in London. Lord Sainsbury, married to a onetime ballet dancer, is head of the Royal Opera House.

In the business world, the family owns more than half of J. Sainsbury P.L.C., which operates a chain of several hundred stores in England and Wales selling groceries, household goods and do-it-yourself merchandise. In 1989, Sainsbury's sales of better than $9 billion earned the company undisputed standing as Britain's largest operator of grocery stores.

Sir John Sainsbury in September 1981.

For all their social prominence and the respect they commanded as business managers, the Sainsburys could well see a challenging decade in the 1990s. Given the approach of European economic unity in 1992, many observers thought British retailing in general was likely to face a stern test from expansion-minded, cost-cutting competitors on the Continent. At the same time, the Sainsburys had started another high-stakes venture. In 1987, they extended their reach beyond Olde England to New England with the acquisition of Shaw's supermarkets, an operation consisting of about sixty stores in the northeastern United States. That took them into territory where some of their counterparts in British retailing had previously met with less than total success.

David J. Sainsbury in July 1980.

GUSTAVO CISNEROS

From left to right: Mr. and Mrs. Gustavo Cisneros, Ambassador George Landau and his wife, and David Rockefeller at the Center for International Relations in New York in 1986.

Among the countless family fortunes of the world that can be traced to modest origins, few had a less imposing start than that of the Venezuelan Cisneros clan. To be specific, in 1929, the first rolling stock of the Organizacion Diego Sisneros was a bus fashioned from the remnants of an old dump truck. A little more than a decade later, however, the business began traveling in considerably fancier style when it landed the Venezuelan franchise for the soft drink Pepsi. The company went on to become one of the biggest independent Pepsi distributors anywhere.

This set an example that was to be followed repeatedly as the business kept expanding and passed in time from one generation of Cisneroses to the next. The family bought up Venezuelan stores once operated by the U.S.-based company Sears Roebuck, and obtained exclusive local rights to such other North American names as Apple Computer together with franchises for food giants such as Pizza Hut and Burger King. Meanwhile, the company was also prospering on its own account, building up a dominant Venezuelan presence in supermarkets and other types of retailing, along with many other businesses.

Today the family is still finding new opportunities in its native land: a big

Gustavo and Patty
Cisneros.

investment in an aluminum processing
venture, for instance. As Henry
Cisneros, who is in his mid-forties and
now runs the company with his brother
Ricardo, told *Forbes* magazine,
"Venezuela is really like Korea was ten
or fifteen years ago." At the same time,
however, it has widened its horizons on
an international scale over the past
decade with forays into places such as
London and New York.

In Britain the company bought,
among other things, a package of real
estate that included Paternoster Square,
a commercial complex adjoining St.
Paul's Cathedral in London. On the
other side of the Atlantic it snapped up
the Spalding sports goods company,
with designs on worldwide markets for
such products as tennis balls. Gustavo
also polished up his image as a globe-
trotting tycoon by buying a Fifth
Avenue residence that was formerly the
property of Richard Nixon.

Baron Hans Heinrich
Thyssen-Bornemisza with
his fifth wife, Carmen
"Tita" Cervera, a former
Miss Spain, in 1988.

If you're looking for a true storybook billionaire, may we suggest the Baron, known to intimates as "Heinie". Picture him, if you will, in his Swiss villa on Lake Lugano, protected by a team of bodyguards, with a white Rolls-Royce sitting out in the driveway. The woman with him is his fifth wife, Carmen, or "Tita," a former Miss Spain who once was featured in the pages of the German edition of *Penthouse*.

Then there is his art collection, worth $1 billion or more by itself and a worthy challenger to the assemblage in the hands of the British royal family. In 1988 the baron helped keep the world art market jumping by paying $24 million for Gaugin's much-admired "Mata Mua." A mere whisper about the baron's possible future plans for the collection can attract supplicant emissaries from governments and museums all over the world. At last count it embraced some 1,400 works, more than half of them slated for a ten-year period on loan in Madrid.

Mata Mua by Paul Gaugin, part of the baron's art collection.

Though the art alone meets any standard of world-class wealth, it is by no means all there is to the family fortune. The baron's son George oversees the shipping-container, farm-machinery and other enterprises of the Thysenn-Bornemisza Group, whose annual revenues have surpasses $3 billion. The business is descended from a steel and shipping empire assembled by the baron's grandfather and nurtured by his father, who brought the base of operations to Switzerland from Hungary in 1939.

Security-conscious as he must be, the baron is not particularly jealous of his privacy. For decades much of his villa has been open to the public, providing an accommodation to the art lover or the just plain curious tourist. He is, however, reported to have at least one eccentricity – daily consultations with a fortuneteller.

Above: Baron Hans Heinrich Thyssen-Bornemisza poses in front of a Picasso painting in the Modern Art Museum of Paris in 1985.

Left: the millionaire steel magnate in 1954 with his second wife, British fashion model Nina Dyer.

The baron and his third wife, former British fashion model Fiona Campbell-Walter, on their honeymoon in Italy in 1956.

SAMUEL AND DONALD NEWHOUSE

So you think your taxes give you a headache? Consider the case of the Newhouse family, which spent about ten years battling with the U.S. government's Internal Revenue Service over a little matter of $550 million or so. In early 1990 a court ruled in favor of the Newhouses, helping to enhance their standing as owners of one of the richest and most prestigious communications empires in the world. If nothing else, the dispute demonstrated how difficult it can be to place an exact value at any given time on a large fortune. By various estimates, the Newhouses are worth $5 billion or more.

S.I. Newhouse Jr. (left) and Donald Newhouse escorting their mother Mitzi after attending funeral services for their father, publisher Samuel I. Newhouse.

Right: S.I. Newhouse, 1974. Below: the late Mitze Newhouse, in an undated Cecil Beton photo from *Vogue* magazine. A patron of the arts and a leading figure in women's fashions, she died in 1989 at age 87.

The New Yorker magazine's trademark, Mr Eustace Tilley (left), appeared on the cover of the first issue in 1925 and was still featured in this 1949 issue. S.I. Newhouse, Jr., purchased the magazine in 1985.

S.I. Newhouse, Jr., (below, third from left) at a 1984 anniversary party for the Newhouse Communications Center held in Syracuse. His brother Donald is on the extreme left of the picture.

The argument involved the value of the estate left by Samuel Newhouse Sr., father of "Si" and Donald, when he died in 1979. Among those family jewels were more than two dozen newspapers and five radio stations, as well as Conde Nast, publisher of *Vogue* and other magazines. Today the family's Advance Publications and Newhouse Broadcasting also have cable television interests; blue-chip magazines like the *New Yorker*, *Parade* and *Vanity Fair*, and Random House in book publishing.

The first link in that chain was forged in 1922 when Sam Newhouse, a child of East European immigrants to the United States, transformed himself from law clerk to newspaper owner. His acquisition was the *Staten Island Advance*,

The first issue of Glamour magazine (below left) in April 1939 featured the movie star Ann Sheridan on its cover. In 1989 the magazine celebrated its fiftieth anniversary by featuring four super-models on its cover (below). Reading clockwise from the top left-hand corner, they were Christie Brinkley, Beverly Johnson, Kim Alexis and Cheryl Tiegs.

S.I. Newhouse Jr., in
1985.

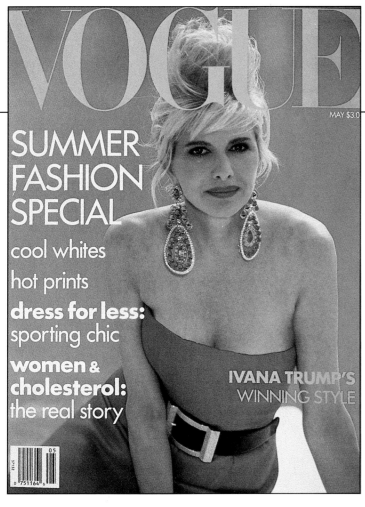

Conde Nast publications owned by Si and Donald Newhouse include *Bride's*, *Glamour*, *Gentleman's Quarterly*, *Gourmet*, *House and Garden*, *Mademoiselle*, *Self*, *Traveler*, *Woman*, *Vanity Fair*, and *Vogue*.

published in a borough of New York City that is best known for the ferry that links it with the celebrated skyscrapers of Manhattan. Nearly seventy years later, the family retains sole ownership of the business for which Si and Donald share the total responsibility. Donald runs the newspaper and television concerns while Si manages the magazine and book publishing companies. The Newhouses are in the spotlight of world media attention, as they own one of the largest magazine and book publishing empires in the world.

Millions of people buy their products, and they may be ten times as rich as some other billionaires who make the headlines and television newscasts every day. But hardly anybody knows anything about octogenarian Forrest E. Mars Sr. and his three children, whose $12.5 billion candy fortune puts them high on the list of the wealthiest private families in the world.

That's just the way the Marses want it. While Mars Incorporated spends hundreds of millions of dollars each year to advertise its brand names worldwide, the family vehemently resists any press coverage of its private lives. A case in point: *Fortune* magazine reports that Forrest Sr. once called the police to repel the advances of two of its reporters who telephoned his home. The sketchy accounts that do surface portray him as a harsh, hard-driving autocrat feared by his employees and family along with his competitors. Whatever their personal feelings about their father,

the Mars children have continued his penchant for privacy and many other of his ways.

There is little in the family history that bespeaks much of comfort or gentle intimacy. Forrest Sr.'s parents, Frank and Ethel Mars, experienced a series of failures in the candy business before the family struck chocolate gold in 1923 with the first appearance of the Milky Way bar. The years that followed brought such other big winners as Snickers and M&Ms. Early on, Frank is said to have set Forrest up in the British candy business in order to keep him far removed from the center of activity in the United States. But Forrest was back by 1940, and twenty-four years later had won full control of the company.

Mars Incorporated today has branched out into other household-name consumer products – Uncle Ben's rice and Kal Kan pet food. Forrest Sr., who turned over the running of the business to the younger generation in 1973, "retired" to Las Vegas, Nevada, where he started a gourmet candy company.

Some of the candies that have made Mars Inc. a sweet fortune.

KANICHIRO ISHIBASHI

Shojiro Ishibashi, founder of Bridgestone Tire Company.

East began to meet West a long time ago in the annals of this man's Tokyo family, which had amassed a fortune estimated at well over $1 billion by the late 1980s. When Shojiro Ishibashi started a business nearly sixty years ago, he called the enterprise Bridgestone in an anglicized play on his surname ("bashi" for bridge and "ishi" for stone). He brought his children up with forks as well as chopsticks at the dinner table. And Bridgestone, for its part, made a product with a potentially universal market – automobile tires.

Automobile tire manufacturing at Firestone.

Yet, until fairly recently, Bridgestone had achieved most of its success within the borders of Japan, under the stewardship of Shojiro and his son Kanichiro, who took over the helm in 1963 and at the age of seventy held the title of honorary chairman. With all its prosperity, some observers thought Bridgestone was slow to keep pace with Japanese auto manufactures and other types of businesses in conquering markets overseas.

Once the family made its move, however, it did so in grand style, laying out about $2.5 billion to buy the U.S.-based Firestone Tire & Rubber and another $2 billion or thereabouts to modernize and expand its acquisition. That gave it a strong foothold not only in the States, but also in Latin America and Europe. Some $350 million alone was earmarked for a new factory in Tennessee.

That made it plain that the family and its business had ambitious plans for the 1990s. As *Forbes* magazine observed: "Clearly Bridgestone is not content to be the world's No. 3 tiremaker. Goodyear and Michelin, watch out."

Inspecting tires at Bridgestone, the top tire-maker in Japan and third largest worldwide.

As immensely rich and powerful as the Cargill and MacMillan families of Minneapolis, Minnesota, and other points around the globe, may be, chances are you've never heard much about them. Well, that's just fine with the Cargills and the MacMillans, who have never evinced the slightest interest in fame or notoriety.

The company that is the basis of their fortune – Cargill Incorporated, a dominant force in the worldwide grain business and an employer of some 50,000 people – is privately owned, and thus does not have to tell the world how it is doing. Among its competitors, customers and suppliers, it is legendary for its secrecy. In their personal lives, the family members are just as jealous of their privacy. When one MacMillan ended his thirty-year marriage and wed a secretary, according to *Fortune* magazine, the news did not reach the ears of a local gossip columnist until a year later. After extensive digging into the family affairs, *Forbes* magazine came up with this information about another member: "Married. Number of children not known. Residence unknown."

The modern Cargill Incorporated, with annual revenues in the neighborhood of $40 billion, traces its origins to a business established 150 years ago by William Cargill, the son of a Scottish sea captain. The founder's son-in-law, John MacMillan, took charge in the early twentieth century. Today Whitney MacMillan, a grandson of John, is chairman. Whitney's brother Cargill retired in 1988 after fifteen years as an executive vice president.

Whitney has demonstrated a keen interest in international politics. He has been a frequent visitor to the Soviet Union, and served in a group that studied how best the United States might respond to the *glasnost* policy instituted by Mikhail Gorbachev. In one seeming display of a softer, less secretive side, he took the Minneapolis Children's Theater on a trip to Moscow.

Whitney MacMillan, President and Chief Executive Officer of Cargill Incorporated.

ATHINA ROUSSEL

Unlike most of the other people who occupy the pages of this book, Athina apparently isn't a billionaire – at least not yet. But give her time. Barely five years old, she inherited a fortune estimated at $500 million when her mother, Christina Onassis, died November 19, 1988, in Buenos Aires at the age of thirty-seven, the victim of what the authorities said was an accidental overdose of medicine. If the trustees of the Greek family's shipping fortune keep the money invested at even an extremely modest return, Athina will have a billion-plus net worth before she is ready for college.

But will the money buy her happiness? That's the question certain to keep public attention focused in the years ahead on Athina, who has already become one of the youngest individuals ever to occupy the cover of the American magazine *People*. Her mother, married four times, endured a troubled life. Her father, Thierry Roussel, comes equipped, at least in the view of some of the surviving Onassises, with a playboy reputation to go with considerable family wealth of his own.

By *People*'s reckoning, Athina's private world already includes five homes, three bodyguards, two petting zoos and an almost limitless collection of toys. Nevertheless, the magazine reported in early 1989, "her favorite possession is still a shabby plush baby doll she calls Molly."

Thierry Roussel (left), fourth husband of Christina Onassis, arriving at her funeral in Nea Smyrni, Greece, in 1988. Ms. Onassis died of a heart attack at age thirty-seven.

Christina Onassis (above) dancing at a party at the Uruguayan Embassy with Jorge Tohomlkdjoglou.

Athina Roussel, age four, holds her father's hand after his 1990 marriage to Gaby Landhage.

SEIJI AND YOSHIAKI TSUTSUMI

Yasujiro Tsutsumi, father of Seiji and Yoshiaki, is photographed in 1961 on a visit with British Foreign Secretary Sir Alec Douglas- Home in London.

IF these Japanese half brothers (same father, different mothers) ever joined forces, they would be as formidable contenders as anyone for the title "Owners of the World." But fate has cast them as rivals with dramatic differences in style and temperament. The bitterness between them is said to go back to their youth, when Yoshiaki won his father's favor as the more obedient son. On the death of the father, Yasujiro, in 1964, Yoshiaki inherited most of the family assets, including a major railroad and the real estate it owned. Seiji, whose main legacy was an unglamorous department store, has expressed his feelings in lines of poetry such as "I am what I am."

By some reckonings, Yoshiaki is the richest private citizen in the world, with a net worth of $15 billion or more. He has assumed the role of cautious conservator of the family empire, which extends beyond the railroad into construction and other businesses, as well as owning a huge portfolio of stocks. Yoshiaki is also a sportsman – owner of the Seibu Lions baseball team and an investor in golf courses and ski resources – but he disavows any interest in high-risk business games, shying away from borrowing and foreign partnerships.

Seiji, the outsider, has gained a contrasting reputation for the bold business stroke. The store he started out with has grown into a string of one hundred businesses, financed with the help of billions in borrowed money and reaching as far as Scotland, where he and some foreign partners bought a hotel.

The paths of the two Tsutsumis converged a couple of years ago when the Inter-Continental Hotel chain was up for sale. Yoshiaki passed on the deal, saying the price was too high to pay on his own and declining to bid with anybody else. Seiji then jumped in quickly with a winning $2.5 billion bid. To many observers of their long rivalry, the symbolism of that gesture was hard to miss.

THE HSU FAMILY

Y.Z. Hsu.

Money and success in business have proved a means to many ends for Y.Z. Hsu of Taiwan, now approaching the age of eighty. More than half his lifetime ago, he had to move his textile business from Shanghai to Taipei when communist rule came to mainland China. What was then a modest knitting mill has since become a multifaceted enterprise called the Far Eastern Group with annual revenues in the $2 billion range. It is still known as a textile business, but it has extended its operations into chemicals, cement, shipping, department stores and investments.

Hsu's own experiences clearly helped shape his preference for doing things bigger and better. A high school graduate in China, he sought a more advanced education, with a Western element, for the next generation of his family. His son Douglas, for example,

got a graduate degree in business from Columbia University in New York en route to becoming president of Far Eastern Textile. Douglas, in turn, has brought in other young managers with American schooling to try to keep the business competitive in an increasingly international marketplace. Another son, John, holds a doctoral degree and heads the family's Asia Cement Corp.

Y.Z. Hsu has further demonstrated his commitment to causes such as education, health and science by putting some of his wealth and energy to work creating a foundation, setting up a hospital and starting a college specializing in engineering.

Hsu's son Douglas provided a glimpse into the impulse behind all this modernization and change. As he told *Forbes* magazine: "If our competitors do not move in the same way, they will be left behind."

GODFRIED BRENNINKMEYER AND FAMILY

The Dutch, famous for accomplishing big things within a small space, can claim several family fortunes that rival the immense wealth of their royal household. Perhaps the number one contender is the Brenninkmeyer family of Amsterdam, who have a retailing and real estate empire that extends to just about every corner of the non-communist world.

While Queen Beatrix is a public figure, the Brenninkmeyers are private, private, private. Though their business traces its origins back almost a hundred and fifty years, they have managed to keep curious outsiders from learning much about its value or profitability. To further that aim, for example, they run their British operations as an unlimited company. That means that they forego an important measure of protection many other businesses routinely seek to restrict their vulnerability to legal or financial claims against the business. But it lets them avoid the necessity of much public reporting on the state of their finances.

So it is that expert estimates of the Brenninkmeyers' wealth vary significantly. *Fortune* magazine put it at $4 billion; *Forbes* assessed it as "at least $5 billion, and probably much more than that."

Brenninkmeyer stores can be found in Hong Kong, Japan, Brazil, France, Switzerland, West German, Britain and the United States. The U.S. business alone comprises eight separate store chains, including Womans World Co. in California and Eastern Mountain Sports, which is headquartered in New Hampshire. In Britain, the family's one-hundred-plus C&A clothing stores are estimated to ring up annual sales of close on $1 billion.

HANS AND GAD RAUSING

The formidable fortune of these brothers is neatly wrapped up in Tetra Pak Group, a packaging company founded by their father nearly forty years ago. Tetra Pak's prize product, a sterile vacuum container for perishable liquids such as milk and fruit juice, enjoys a vast and growing market in Europe and many other corners of the globe. The business's simple motto: "A package should save more than it costs."

Beyond that, however, the Rausings' story gets more complicated. For example, there's the matter of nationality. The Rausings, raised in Sweden, live in London and Sussex, England. Tetra Pak, registered in the Netherlands, has its headquarters in Lausanne.

Then there is the question of just how much Tetra Pak and the brothers, who are its sole owners, are worth. Yearly sales now of Tetra Paks are reckoned at about $3 billion, but profit figures are hard to come by. The company has reached a degree of maturity in Europe, where it has about 60% of the liquid-packaging business. What of its potential, though, in China, where it has been enthusiastically received? or in the Soviet Union, where the Rausings have discussed possible ventures? Or the United States, where acceptance of the package has been slower in coming to date?

Working with such an imprecise picture, researchers on the subject have variously pegged the brothers' fortune at $3.5 billion to $7 billion. Given the increasingly international marketplace for consumer goods as the 1990s began, even the latter figure may be low.

GERALD GROSVENOR

Gerald Grosvenor, the sixth Duke of Westminster and a descendant of William the Conqueror, holds sway over a string of family real estate holdings. A partial list would include, in the British Isles alone, a 13,000-acre estate; properties in the fashionable Belgravia and Mayfair districts of London, and forest and farmland in England and Scotland.

Beyond Britain, Grosvenor International Holdings Ltd., which is based in Vancouver, British Columbia, owns several dozen properties in locales ranging from Australia and Hawaii to San Francisco and Chicago. A prime focus of big and growing investments is Vancouver itself, which a GIH official approvingly described to *Forbes* magazine as "Canada's biggest warm-weather port."

The value of real estate is notoriously hard to guage with any precision, especially when it is prime property that hasn't changed hands for many years. That goes a long way toward explaining why the Grosvenor assets have been estimated to be worth anywhere from $3 billion to $7 billion. To complicate the situation, GIH has embarked on many of its ventures with partners and co-owners, including a number of British and American pension funds, whose managers have become keenly enamored of real estate investments in recent years.

Like many a landlord, Grosvenor has had some disagreements with his tenants, over matters ranging from rights to purchase housing to the feeding of birds. To balance the accounts somewhat, he took charge of a campaign to help poor villages in Britain.

Gerald Cavendish Grosvenor, sixth Duke of Westminster, and reputedly Britain's richest man.

Chapter 5

Self-Made

SAM WALTON

Forbes magazine listed Sam Walton as the richest man in America in 1984.

Everybody knows that all the big money that matters in the United States spends its time on the coasts – most particularly, in California on the Pacific, New York and Washington on the Atlantic side. For a long time, as the movers and shakers jetted back and forth between these outposts of influence, they neglected to look down and see what Sam Walton was accomplishing in the vast expanse between.

By now, however, they can no longer overlook his name, or the $9 billion fortune he has built from almost a standing start within the last thirty years. Walton's Wal-Mart Stores may well be the biggest retailer in America, having outstripped such old-line stalwarts as Sears Roebuck, K-Mart and J.C. Penney. And with all that, Walton still retains the persona of the simple rural American, motoring around in a weather-beaten pickup truck with two hunting dogs for company, and insisting that everybody call him Sam.

Walton's first discount store opened for business in Rogers, Arkansas, in

Above: Walton promoting the buying of American products as the possible answer to the country's trade deficit in 1986.

Sam Walton (left), founder of Wal-Mart Stores, comparing a foreign-made chair to the patio chairs his company makes. "Now which is the better chair?" he asked. "The one made in America, of course."

1962. Now there are more than 1,300 of them, selling a variety of more than 50,000 products that range from shoes to small appliances. For all its unassuming style and its just-folks clientele, Wal-Mart is a sophisticated business with a satellite communications system and muscles it knows how to flex. As an executive of a manufacturer that sells goods to Wal-Mart once remarked, "They talk softly, but they have piranha hearts."

Walton is past the age of seventy, and he no longer dominates his huge business the way he did in its early days. But that fits with Wal-Mart's long-standing system of emphasizing the initiative of individual store managers and, indeed, of each individual employee – or "associate," as Walton long ago dubbed them. If it had been written as fiction, his success story might strain credulity. But since it is fact, he is entitled to say, "If people believe in themselves, it is truly amazing what they can accomplish."

Sam Walton doing the hula in front of Merrill Lynch headquarters in New York, keeping his word to do so if his company made a pre-tax net profit of 8 percent in 1984.

LIEM SIOE LIONG

This tycoon in Jakarta, Indonesia, knows the many benefits, and a few of the drawbacks, of having a friend in high places. Born into a peasant family in China in 1916, Liem moved to Java in 1938 and joined his uncle in a small mercantile business.

When Indonesia sought and won independence from the Dutch after World War II, Liem became a major supplier of arms and sustenance to the nationalists. In addition, he forged a friendship with an officer named Suharto, who was to become president of the country.

As Suharto's financial backer, he attained a powerful position at the heart of Indonesia's economy. By one recent calculation, Liem controlled a one-fourth interest in the country's biggest bank, two-thirds of a flour milling concern and almost half of a large cement company. His other enterprises included a monopoly position in the trade in cloves, an ancient staple of the Indonesian spice trade, and majority ownership of a financial and telecommunications conglomerate based in Hong Kong. According to *Forbes* magazine, the latter business "is widely assumed to be a conduit for flight capital" seeking safe havens around the world from political change or instability. All told, Liem's fortune has been estimated at $2 billion.

His wealth and connections, however, have not always been enough to insulate Liem from controversy. In fact, they have engendered criticism and resentment among some Indonesians, who contend that he gets unjustified favors from the government. In his mid-70s, Liem seemed to have set himself the new challenge, in *Forbes'* words, of "working on the family's image by bringing more Chinese and Indonesians into new management and ownership positions."

H ROSS PEROT

H. Ross Perot (right and below right) at a reception/dinner at New York's Waldorf-Astoria Hotel in 1987, at which he was given the Raoul Wallenberg Award.

The Dallas-Fort Worth Airport, with *Concorde* among those planes on the ground.

Before he had amassed more than a small fraction of his $3 billion fortune, Texan Ross Perot had already made his mark in the world doing things his own way.

There was the time, for example, in the early 1960s when Perot fulfilled his annual quota as a computer salesman of International Business Machines in just a few weeks. Rejecting suggestions that he take a long vacation, and frustrated in his search for ways to stretch himself, he started his own business, Electronic Data Systems, selling information-processing services to companies and government departments that didn't have their own computers. His EDS holdings, worth well over $1 billion in 1970, lost all but about $100 of their value over the next four years in a severe bear market.

Perot ran into another reversal about the same time when he tried without success to build a new financial empire from the remains of several down-and-out investment firms on Wall Street. "I was trying to farm where there was no rain," he later conceded.

That hardly quelled his willingness to take risks, however. In 1979, as the U.S government was struggling to secure the freedom of hostages in the Middle East, he financed and led a successful private mission to get two EDS

Perot sharing a laugh with friend Nancy Brinker during a 1987 roast held in his honor by the Dallas Press Club – for which those attending paid $60 to $500 a plate.

employees out of an Iranian prison.

EDS once again commanded a price of better than $1 billion when Perot sold it to General Motors in 1984. Two years later he and GM parted company after a noisy demonstration of the incompatibility of an idiosyncratic entrepreneur with an entrenched bureaucracy. Still undaunted, Perot invested in new computer projects and set out with his son to build an airport near Fort Worth, Texas.

By now it was clear that Perot was driven by far more than a desire to get rich. Indeed, as he warned an audience at the Harvard Business School, money alone often buys more worries than satisfaction. "Go to a yacht basin any place in the world," he said. "Nobody is smiling, and I'll tell you why: Something broke that morning. The generator's out – the microwave oven doesn't work – the captain's gay – the cook's quit. THINGS just don't mean happiness."

Perot visiting the Bien Hoa prisoner of war camp in Vietnam in 1970.

Dallas computer magnate H. Ross Perot (at left), after arranging for an American-led commando squad to free two of his employees from imprisonment by the Iranians in 1979. With Perot are (from left) Bill Gaylord and Paul Chiapperoni, and Arthur "Bull" Simons, retired U.S. Army colonel.

Electronic Data Systems chairman H. Ross Perot at the control center of the company's information processing center in Auburn Hills, Michigan, in 1985.

LAURENCE AND PRESTON ROBERT TISCH

The Tisch brothers were born and raised in Brooklyn, New York, a fertile breeding ground of American overachievers, and wasted little time demonstrating that they were headed for big things. Older brother Larry, a college graduate at eighteen, and Bob embarked on a real-estate career building and renovating hotels. They then branched out into movie theaters, which eventually led them to control of the basic building block of their $2 billion-plus empire, Loews Corporation.

Their horizons kept expanding as their wealth and prominence increased. Bob put in a stint as Postmaster General of the United States. Names like Bulova, the watch manufacturer, and CNA Financial joined the family stable of businesses. In 1986 they took a great leap forward when Larry grabbed the reins at CBS, a tradition-rich but troubled communications giant that had been the home of such legendary television and radio news figures as Edward R. Murrow and Walter Cronkite. Two years later Bob also was named to the CBS board of directors.

Laurence Tisch (above, center), then president and chief executive officer of CBS Inc., shakes hands with baseball commissioner Peter Ueberroth after acquiring exclusive television rights to the World Series, the National and American League Championship Series, the All-Star Game and twelve regular season games for the four years beginning in 1990.

Laurence Tisch (right) with popular game show host Pat Sajak, shortly after signing him up for a new program in 1988.

Laurence Tisch (on the right) with newscasters Rolland Smith and Mariette Hartley after the première of CBS's "The Morning Program" in 1987.

Jonathan Tisch (on the right), president of Loew's Hotels, and New York City Mayor David Dinkins display the 1991 Grammy Awards jackets, with singer Roberta Flack.

Right: Robert Tisch (on the left), then president of Loew's Hotels, and brother Laurence Tisch, then president and board chairman of the parent company Loew's Theatres Inc., inspecting a model of the Americana Hotel, which opened in New York in 1962.

Below: Robert Tisch in the presidential suite of Loew's Summit Hotel.

Several children have followed in their footsteps – Larry's son Andrew, for example, running Bulova, and Bob's son Jonathan as chief executive of Loews hotels. It is, without question, a family of forceful egos, but its emphasis has been on public-spirited progress rather than mere materialistic rewards. One noteworthy gesture: a gift of $30 million from Larry and Bob to New York University's medical center, now Tisch Hospital.

Larry's views of his position at CBS bespeak a family with a mission. "This is no longer a financial investment for him," a confidante told the New York Times. "He believes that this is an

investment he made for history, for his children, for financial reasons and out of a desire to become a corporate statesman."

Whatever else appeals to the Tisches about a life of wealth and power, self-indulgence does not seem to count for much. Larry and his wife Billie, married since 1948, divide their time between a New York apartment and a weekend home in suburban Rye, New York, that are described as comfortable but far short of lavish. "Your standard of living doesn't change after the first million," Larry once observed. "I don't want to become possessed by my possessions."

From left to right: Robert Tisch; Saul Farber, dean of the N.Y.U. Medical School; John Brademas, president of N.Y.U.; Laurence Tisch; and John Murphy, board chairman of the N.Y.U. Medical Center.

WARREN BUFFETT

Warren Buffett, board chairman and chief executive officer of Berkshire Hathaway.

Yes, one can get rich investing in stocks. At least one can if one is Warren Buffett, a plain-spoken, bespectacled native of the American Midwest who turned an affinity for financial analysis into a fortune worth more than $3.5 billion while seldom straying far from home. What's more, in an age of corporate raiders and computer-program traders, Buffett earned his money, and affectionate sobriquet "the wizard of Omaha," investing the old-fashioned way – for the long term. In the process, he built his Berkshire Hathaway Corporation into one of the quirkiest and yet most successful "conglomerates" in business history. Berkshire's various operating entities make or sell candy, encyclopedias, furniture, uniforms, newspapers and vacuum cleaners, among other endeavours, all equally simple but profitable. Berkshire has also made major investments in such independent names as Coca- Cola, the Washington Post Company and Capital Cities-ABC.

Buffett owns a little less than half of Berkshire's stock, and the rest is traded

Above left: the bottle used by Coca-Cola today stands by the prototype of the first Coke bottle in a case in the world headquarters for the firm in Atlanta, Georgia.

Left: Warren Buffett (on the right), chairman of Berkshire Hathaway, joins Thornton Bradshaw, former chairman of RCA, in honoring Katharine Graham, board chairman of the Washington Post Co.

on the New York Stock Exchange. His popularity with his fellow shareholders can be grasped through some simple arithmetic. If you had invested $12,000 in Berkshire in 1965 it would have been worth as much as $8.9 million twenty-four years later.

Most of the people who operate at or anywhere close to Buffett's level in the world financial arena are viewed as sharks out to tear apart a vulnerable victim. But many a management at the headquarters of a corporation has welcomed or even sought out Buffett the investor as a "white squire," a friendly source of patient, non-interfering capital. Buffett has shrewdly capitalized on this unique status to make some deals on what could only be called extremely advantageous terms.

Perhaps his closet foray into flamboyance was playing the part of a bartender on a television soap opera. Otherwise, his taste in "luxuries" runs to such indulgences as Cherry Coke.

Buffett at the new York Stock Exchange, flanked by NYSE specialist James J. Maguire (right) of Henderson Brothers, and David L. Domijan, senior vice president of the Stock Exchange.

KENKICHI NAKAJIMA

Workers in Kenkichi Nakajima's Heiwa factory north of Tokyo assemble Pachinko machines, which are like western pinball machines.

For anyone who is still caught up in the image of modern Japan as a culture of all work and no play, the story of this man's self-propelled rise to wealth is a true eye-opener. Make no mistake – Nakajima, in the classic mold of the twentieth-century entrepreneur, toiled long and hard to earn *Fortune* magazine's billing in the late 1980s as the richest person in a very rich land. But he built his fortune on a foundation of games – specifically pachinko, which is analogous to the Western game of pinball.

Nakajimo was born in Korea, but came to Japan as a student and put in time during World War II working in a defense plant. Once the global hostilities were over, he cast about for a way to make his mark in some arena that had nothing to do with war, and found it manufacturing pachinko machines. In case that wasn't enough to make his intentions crystal clear, he named his company Heiwa, or "Peace." By 1988 Heiwa was bringing in more than $350 million a year in revenues. When Japanese investors were given the chance to invest in Heiwa stock, they bid up its price nearly 70% in the first day it was traded. Since Nakajima and

Kenkichi Nakajima,
photographed in his office
in 1990.

his family had retained about seven-eighths' ownership of the business, that catapulted them, with holdings worth something in excess of $3 billion, to new heights among the world's wealthiest people.

Nakajima, more than eligible to "retire" as he was nearing seventy, showed no interest in standing pat with the winning hand he had dealt himself. Much of his energy still went into maintaining Heiwa's success by keeping up to date with the latest high-technology innovations in pachinko equipment. At the same time, he engaged French architects to help create

a new landmark of leisure: what he hoped would be the top golf course in Japan.

From his own point of view, he could see definite limits to the value of wealth for its own sake. Once a person has acquired a nice place to live and a few million dollars in other assets, he told *Forbes*, there isn't much more that money can buy. "You can't go around wearing a coat made of pure gold, nor can you eat food ten times a day," he said. "In fact, it's probably better not to have too much." And on the permanence and reliability of a personal fortune: "Money is a wanderer."

Y C WANG

Legends abound of the fortunes some enterprising people have made using ideas or opportunities rejected by others – the movie script deemed unfilmable, or the product that market researchers determined would "never sell." Such is the story of Y.C. Wang and his family in Taipei, Taiwan, and their Formosa Plastics Group, whose annual world wide revenues have approached $6 billion.

In the 1950s, it seems, a group of Americans on a mission of economic aid came pitching a venture producing resins – a versatile building block in the chemical and plastics industries that finds its way into products as diverse as adhesives, synthetic fibers and billiard balls. A good many of Taiwan's leading businesses declined the offer as unpromising. W.C. Wang, who at that time was the proprietor of a lumber business, said yes. Today Formosa Plastics is described as the biggest diversified company in Taiwan and the number one producer of resins in the world.

Its success didn't win Formosa Plastics universal friendship. For one thing, the company has been a target of opposition from Taiwan's environmentalists. It has also seen some

manufacturing businesses it supplies leave Taiwan for other locales in Southeast Asia.

These and other circumstances have helped encourage the company to seek a big part of its future in the United States, where it has more than a dozen plants in operation and others planned or under construction. Presumably, that means new places to see for Y.C. Wang, whose life, even now that he is in his seventies, is so closely tied to his work that he lives in a penthouse at the company headquarters and calls it a vacation when he travels to other Formosa Plastic facilities.

Y.C. Wang, Chairman of the Formosa Plastics Group.

TSAI WAN-LIN

Tsai Wan-lin, chairman of Taiwan's Cathay Life Insurance Co.

Hard work can take you far. But it also helps if you apply your efforts toward realizing the right ideas in the right place at the right time.

That principle helps explain the long journey of this Taiwan tycoon from a childhood on a humble rice farm to his control of an empire worth $10 billion or more. Tsai and his late brother started small, operating a fruit and vegetable stand and subsequently manufacturing soy sauce. Their horizons expanded into real estate, construction, finance and other fields. Today the jewel in the crown of Tsai's Yuan-lin Group is majority ownership of a fast-growing life insurance company called Cathay Life, the value of whose stock more than doubled in the late 1980s.

Life insurance proved to be a highly successful idea because the prosperity of Taiwan's population was increasing rapidly, putting more and more people in income brackets that merited their protection against untimely death. It also helped that insurance was one Western product that gained sharply increased acceptance as Taiwanese affluence spread. To top it all off, there was a boom in values on the Taipei Stock Exchange, where Cathay Life became a favorite with investors because of its seemingly boundless business prospects.

Despite the grand scale of his success, Tsai hasn't changed his personal values much. He shuns interviews with the press, and lives a good deal of the time in an unpretentious apartment close to his headquarters. Leisure- time indulgences? Now and then a weekend game of golf. *Fortune* magazine reported that he declined to buy himself a Rolls Royce because, in the words of an associate, "he doesn't want to show off."

LI KA-SHING

Li Ka-Shing speaking to the Hong Kong press in 1990.

As money flows around the world, a lot of it passes sooner or later through one little eyelet on the globe – the British colony of Hong Kong, a strategically located port at the southern edge of mainland China. Probably no one sees more of this money than Li Ka-shing, a businessman and investor in his early sixties, who is widely accorded the title of Hong Kong's richest individual.

At the age of fourteen, Li went to work supporting his family as a toy salesman after his father died. Less than ten years later he had started a plastics business under the name Cheung Kong that has since grown into one of Hong Kong's biggest businesses. In the late 1970s, he also gained control of Hutchison Whampoa, a trading company with interests in such diverse fields as electric power, oil and telecommunications.

While money never sat still for very long in Hong Kong, it has been moving faster and faster in recent years as business managers and investors look ahead to 1998, when the colony is scheduled to revert to Chinese control. There are few historical precedents for such a head-on meeting of communism and capitalism.

Faced with this prospect, much

"smart money" has already fled Hong Kong. Its stock market has seesawed wildly. At the center of this storm, Li has taken steps to position his fortune so that he can both counter any peril and take advantage of any opportunity. On the one hand, he seems convinced that Chinese leaders will recognize how much their country stands to benefit from the financial and commercial clout of Hong Kong. He retains huge holdings in shipping terminals and other real estate, and is making plans for other enormous ventures in transportation and cable television.

At the same time, his bets have been hedged in real estate holdings and other activities elsewhere – most notably in Canada. He is said to have long since salted away large personal assets in the safe harbors of the United States, Singapore and British Columbia. It is also safe to speculate that he has met a Swiss banker or two along the way.

If Hong Kong prospers into the twenty-first century then Li is likely to share in the bounty. If not, he appears to have done his best to build himself a safety net.

The Whampoa building was built in Hong Kong by Li Ka-Shing and houses shops, restaurants and a health club within its boat shape.

KENNETH COLIN IRVING AND FAMILY

Canadian millionaire
Kenneth Colin Irving in
1987.

Many of the world's wealthiest people spread their assets far and wide, crossing the boundaries set by politics, geography, cultural differences or the market confines for any single line of business. This practice, known as diversification, is prompted by nothing more elaborate than the popular adage, "Don't put all your eggs in one basket."

The opposite approach, which might be called concentration, is employed with a vengeance in the Canadian province of New Brunswick by the Irving family – the patriarch Kenneth, now in his nineties; his sons James, Arthur and John, and their children as well. "The Irvings ARE New Brunswick," asserted *Fortune* magazine. Added one Canadian investment

manager, "It's one of the last feudal states in the world."

To see how this might work, consider all the types of routine commerce that might take place within the Irving empire, estimated to be worth $5 billion to $6 billion. An Irving-owned truck traverses some of the family's three-million-plus acres of timberland to pick up pulp from an Irving mill. On its way toward the coast, it stops for a fill-up of fuel at an Irving service station that is supplied by an Irving refinery. At its final destination, the pulp will be used for paperwork at the Irving's St. John shipyard, where work continues on a multibillion-dollar contract from the Canadian navy. If a mishap should befall the truck along the way, other

Kenneth Colin Irving, photographed in 1977 in front of a map showing the Irving Industries fleet of oil tankers, lumber transports, and newsprint ships – the largest privately-owned fleet flying the Canadian flag.

New Brunswick residents will get the news from a newspaper, TV or radio station owned by, sure enough, the Irvings.

The empire all this represents grew from a single gas station that Kenneth began operating in the 1920s. A couple of years ago the Irvings bought what looked like it might be a similar seed – a station in New Hampshire. Now that they had crossed the U.S. border, observers wondered, what limits did they see?

Kenneth Colin Irving (center) in front of a plaque honoring his reforestation project in New Brunswich, Canada.

BILL GATES

Billionaire computer genius Bill Gates, founder of Microsoft, photographed in 1989.

If you were going to give a party for the richest and the brainiest people in the world, you would need two guest lists. At least one name, however, might be a candidate for both – William Henry Gates III, renowned as a computer genius and probably the youngest billionaire who ever lived.

The original script of his life called for Gates to follow in the footsteps of his father, a highly successful lawyer in Seattle, Washington. He began to change course as early as the age of thirteen, when he wrote his first computer program – the set of instructions and procedures under which information processing equipment operates. At nineteen he dropped out of a pre-law curriculum at Harvard to start a company called

Photographed in 1984, age thirty-one, William Gates, founder and chairman of Microsoft, became the first billionaire in the personal computer business, in 1987.

Microsoft, with a cohort named Paul Allen.

Scarcely a decade later Microsoft, whose products include the basic programs used with International Business Machines personal computers, sold a part interest in itself to the public through an offering of stock. As the price of the shares soared, the approximately 40% stake in the company that Gates kept climbed past $1 billion in value.

In some superficial ways Gates might strike a stranger as an archetypical "computer nerd," with his intense manner, his wiry build, his spectacles and the freckles on his face. But by all accounts, any colleague or competitor who expects him to be a meek sort of character is soon disabused of that idea. Those who deal with him regularly describe the experience as a ferocious contest of energy, will and intellect. In the words of *Fortune* magazine, "Gates is no laid-back West Coast charmer. At Microsoft headquarters, mellowness is in short supply."

Aside from a comfortable home and a penchant for fast cars and boats, Gates has accumulated few trappings of the lavish life. A bachelor known to consume his off-hours reading on a wide range of subjects, he has said his plans for the 1990s don't differ much from what he has being doing so far: "My work is my primary contribution."

Bill Gates (right), chairman of Microsoft, with John Sculley, chairman of Apple Computer, Inc., when they announced production of a new compact disc for the Apple Macintosh.

The campus of the corporate headquarters of Microsoft in Redmond, Washington.

Overleaf: Microsoft computer software products on the assembly line at the manufacturing plant in Bothell, Washington.